MY FATHER

THE

CANTOR

Nom de plume: Lena Rose

Please direct all correspondence to:
1100 Minor Avenue, #218
Seattle, WA 98101
lena7rose@gmail.com

Rose, Lena
My Father the Cantor: Faith's Glory Along My Journey to Empowerment
ISBN 978-0-578-55340-5

1. Biography & Autobiography / Personal Memoirs
2. Biography & Autobiography / Religious

First edition published February 2020

Book design by Bryan Tomasovich at The Publishing World

Printed in the United States
Distributed by Ingram

MY FATHER

THE

CANTOR

Faith's Glory Along
My Journey to Empowerment

a memoir by Lena Rose

In Remembrance of My Dearest Brother

Warren

Forever Present Your Splendor

In the harshly lit hospital he was disquieted amidst the activity. The air stifling, a taste of nausea upon his tongue, he could not ignore his heart's pronounced throbbing. While ambulance attendants rushed victims to emergency, he could no more divert his tearing eyes from this scene than be oblivious to the stone panic shown on the faces of loved ones awaiting the ultimate word. *Will they survive?*

As he passed patients along the corridor navigating their walks and in wheelchairs, hearing cries and moaning from those bedridden, he had to return his focus to a singular purpose, an expected destination.

A family whom he knew well from the congregation had requested he visit in their time of need.

During thirty-one years he had braved many such instances, driven by his compassion to give solace to the suffering. He withheld his own sadness while witnessing those sick and dying, extending his wisdom and comfort, prayers and optimism, yet carrying the awareness of how completely powerless he truly was in predicting the future.

In silence he could not help but be skeptical about prayers actually abating the final outcome. Due to life experience and advanced intellect he grappled with a persistent dichotomy: the practice of religion as absolute for belief and the philosophical debate whether destiny is manifested versus fate. Further, his manner's complexity leaned towards the pragmatic tackling of life's challenges, saving for the pulpit his emphasis on spirituality.

He could only imagine the family's heartache in the face of serious illness. Yet he prevailed in his leadership role proudly, one he may not have envisioned because of his humble beginnings.

♥   ♥

To claim herself the offspring of royalty or notoriety would be attractive. Absent such genealogy, she counted on her parentage hinting of a premise to extraordinary.

I'm a self-made woman. She felt this fitting.

She had perceived early in her life the necessity for hastening her knowledge, appreciating her views on world affairs, cultivating her flair for fashion, the varietal arts, her craftiness with cooking and horticulture, to affirming that most essential of elements within her character's quality, nurtured insightfulness guiding her wisdom.

PART ONE

PART ONE

CHAPTER 1

My paternal grandfather, Woolf, was born in Russia in 1880 but would renounce his citizenship for that of his new homeland of Lithuania. Just shy of age twenty-one in 1901, he was already married with his first child. At the time, Lithuania was a sovereign nation with the USSR on the border. Dire times, however, were forewarning with its fall to Russia's dominance. So great was Woolf's concern for his family's welfare. The United Kingdom beckoned.

London's East End had become a most welcoming district to a diverse cultural and ethnic population. A large segment of *Ashkenazi* Jews (Central and Eastern Europe) and those from the Iberian Peninsula (*Sephardic*) settled there. If perceived as a lower socioeconomic class, it was of little deterrence because the location would satisfy their daily necessities while relishing freely in the enrichment of their faithful Orthodox covenant. Fathers diligently worked their trades while mothers were responsible for making a Jewish home. Unified, all would ensure that their children followed their elder's practices, while commitment to their education propelled promises for success as adults, their pride uplifted through the bond of heritage.

Woolf received an ultra-Orthodox upbringing which influenced his desiring to become a *Chazan* (Cantor), the pious chanter of Jewish liturgy upon the synagogue pulpit shared by the rabbi. He likely accepted he would take on this honorable post in the path of his father because it was generationally assumed.

He earned his keep as a tailor's machinist while his and wife Eva's offspring were plentiful—three girls, Sarah, Esther and Rachel, and three boys, Joe, Jack and Mick.

One evening, the boys were carousing in the yard. As Eva leaned her head out of an upstairs window calling them in for dinner, suddenly she felt the blow of its frame slam her head. Stunned momentarily, she could not have concern about the soreness she felt as there was much to do before the evening was done. She woke the following morning and made her way down to a local public bath, a therapeutic regimen she had found most enjoyable in her home country.

Unbeknownst to her, she sustained a concussion, and while relaxed in the steamy water she passed out and drowned.

Woolf was grief stricken. Adding to his burden was a house full of kids and the daunting task of searching for a new bride to manage the home. Desperate, he realized his second pick had not disclosed her agenda. A shrew, she shamed Woolf, forcing his children to live elsewhere with other relatives, to enable her four children residing in the house. Woolf's unhappiness was released only when she died of an illness three years later.

Woolf would not stand to be without his children for a moment longer than absolutely necessary. Still, he was gun shy at the prospect of a third marriage. He would not accept just any caretaker in the house but a warm soul to refresh his love and someone his children could emulate.

Woolf met Ethel, a woman from Kiev.[1] Some years younger she was a divorcée with two little boys, Dave and Ben. They courted briefly and he quickly realized she was the loving companion with whom he wished to spend his life. His proposal was accepted. Welcoming the bustling household—except Sarah, who had married—the caveat was that Woolf's kids were now in their late teens to early twenties; thus, her responsibility to them less necessary to allow her focusing on her boys. In middle age, Woolf had not expected to father another child; the best laid plans as life is happening. On the twelfth of September in 1928, he and Ethel received the blessing of their son, Mark.[2]

His temperament suggested shyness, an introvert; in his youth he was impressionable, though cautious, yet not pigeon-hearted. He desired an

---

1   Ethel had married a Russian soldier who had fought in WWI. A few years after they immigrated to England he left her to resume his military career.

2   Woolf Rosenkrantz altered his surname to its more common derivative, "Rosen," which means "rose" in English.

enlightenment of the limitless beyond the periphery of home. Within the cover of books he satisfied a voracious appetite for a variety of disciplines, some of which were philosophy, psychology, literature and astrophysics.

But a boy, sports further defined his normality. He loved Rugby and was on his school team. His adolescent focus was on bodybuilding, his physicality an asset to the emergence of his well-being while an outlet for frustration. Mind over matter was his approach to masking his naiveté on the subject of the softer sex.

When Germany dropped bombs on London during the Blitz, Mark's petrified parents abandoned their home to urgently seek protection in a bomb shelter. Once it was safe to return they found their property destroyed. All they could afford was a one-room flat, now distanced from their son who had been called into the army to serve two years. Mark prayed they would be well when his tour ended, but when he reunited with them, he found them both suffering from heart disease. During the next two years they would die.

At twenty, Mark had already enough life experience to enable him trusting his strengths in guiding his intrepid path to his future successes. He qualified for attendance at London's prestigious Queen Mary College. Earning his Bachelor's degree in electrical engineering, he would go on to forge a superlative career in aeronautics.

He also would go in pursuit of the avocation carried forth by his father, yet unclear was where he might find his congregation.

Grander horizons called.

CHAPTER 2

The demise of my paternal grandparents before my birth prohibited my knowledge of them and of my ancestry on my father's side.

My family tree on my mother's side extends only as far as my maternal great grandparents, *Bubbe* and *Zayde* Simons.[3] Their home was in Manchester, England where they brought up their daughters, Ada and Leah, with their Orthodox Jewish traditions. When it came time for them to marry, Leah was betrothed to Sam, Ada to Barney, they the Goldstone brothers.

Leah and Sam had three sons—Sammy, Louis and Hymie—and a daughter, Matilda, who would be known as "Dolly." Ada, too, had given birth to her daughter, Marion, all subsequently residing in the city of Birmingham.

Dolly found the love of her life in Maurice Low. An only child, he was captivated by her vivacious personality. A well-built woman, wanting more than being homemaker excited him. He was a budding entrepreneur desiring her sharing in his own business. They wed. On April 2, 1927 Dolly gave birth to a son, Herbert. On September 9, 1931 Dolly again gave birth to a daughter she named Rita.

Dolly was more the disciplinarian than Maurice who veered towards the tenderhearted, but she gifted Rita with the passion to be herself. As

---

3   With Yiddish integrated as common speech, the term for grandmother and grandfather were used in place of the given name, of which I am unaware.

the youngest female amidst a bunch of male cousins, her confidence was inspired by antics along with compliments. A typical girl, she kept up with the fads and fashion trends. Her social calendar was usually full, her parents trusting she would do right without excessively worrying. They operated from the intention of supportive throughout her upbringing.

Dolly and Maurice were not worldly, yet they held a mutual wisdom of the benefits of unconditional nurturing for the sake of each child's development. Not ones to shy away from displays of affection towards one another, they expressed on their children their belief in their self-worth. They were clearly content, embracing the company of the other in work and play. They enjoyed a drink or two, their nightly ritual a tall glass of Guinness.

Dolly and Maurice, naturally, fostered higher hopes for their son's future; in Judaism, like many other cultures, the male approached often with more consideration. It is fair to say, though, that Rita was pampered, if not spoiled. Due to their attention on Herbert in adolescence, she may have presumed an offense, prompting a jealous reaction towards family and friends. Envisioning her future happy, in the present she could not fully appreciate her blessings.

♥   ♥

Across the crowded floor at a Jewish singles dance Mark spotted Rita coyly flirtatious in conversation. Never had he set his eyes on anyone as beautiful. Her jet black, pinioned hairdo and immaculate appearance caused him to momentarily hesitate. Still, he knew he must make her acquaintance. In his own defense, his tall and handsome physique had been attracting girls. Much more was there for the offering to the right one. In short order, they were smitten, but since Mark was at college for another couple of years they adjusted to some long distance amusement until he came to stay at Rita's parents' house on alternate weekends.

Good looks ran in the family. Cute brother Herbert fell hard for his beauty, Enid. Her family lived in Cardiff, South Wales's capital city. Mark, winning the huge feat of Rita's engagement one month prior to Herbert and Enid's, was to share Herbert's bedroom until the wedding night. Foreseeing the probability that the actual weddings would not occur until employment was secured, the folks insisted on this living arrangement over a period of a year. Back in the day "living together" was actually quite common, no better birds-eye view of the family's internal structure.

Mark and Herbert got along famously, portraying in their relationship a brotherhood. Dolly and Maurice could not have been more elated over the chosen betrothals.

Rita had actually received proposals from two other suitors at the time she accepted Mark's, and she would be sure to often remind him he was her choice. Chuckling in response, Mark could not hear the touch of menace in her tone.

CHAPTER 3

Mark unequivocally exemplified more class and promise. In spite of an upbringing short on wealth, his demonstrated character was immense quality. Sans the unsophisticated cockney accent common to most East Enders he was the best catch. Sharing his long held dreams and determination for adventure enticed, but most appealing was his soft demeanor, resembling that of her father, her womanly charms giving her the edge when needed for purposes of control.

Mark made the ideal husband.

Rita was three years his junior and with all they admired between each other, to include the same birth sign, separated by three days, they seemed perfectly matched. It was at Singers Hill Synagogue that they wed on June 22, 1953, with their destination for a honeymoon in Denmark. As Dolly and Maurice's principal roll was being transferred to Mark, she would become much more a responsibility than he ever imagined.

Rita had brief stints as a Jewish day school teacher and a pharmacist's assistant before marrying, afterwards her sole ambition to be a diligent homemaker. They settled in a ground floor flat a mile from Mark's office. Until he grasped the equitable footing, they determined to hold off plans of starting their own family.

♥   ♥

The secular date was April 3, 1956. On the Jewish calendar the year was 5716, it the eighth day of Passover, which celebrates our Exodus, at God's directive to Moses, out from under decades of untenable slavery in Egypt to freedom in Palestine, the Land of Milk and Honey, where our tribe's spiritual liberation was reclaimed, deservedly.

Rita was about to give birth to her first child, me. In excruciating labor, she was confined to her bed at Dudley Road Hospital in Birmingham, in the same industrial city reminiscent of her own birth, yet quite unlike it otherwise.

How could I conceive of her suffering? That while in the labor ward she was refusing to heed her physician's assertion for a caesarian delivery as the only viable option considering the stress on her weary body? That she was adamant about birthing me naturally, with my father close, and especially, avoiding the unsightly scar?

I was obviously not in any hurry to exit the peaceful solitude of my mother's womb, my activeness a subliminal means by which to allay all worry about my condition.

At almost three weeks past due date, however, my birth was being compromised due to her small pelvis and rising blood pressure. With lives hanging in the balance delicate expert assistance was imperative, a wondrous experience missed on her.

Thank God for Dr. Cope's proficiency. Certainly, her predicament was not my choice, my birth not unlike rescuing a fawn ensnared in a swamp. The procedure, however unfortunate or traumatic, did not need to be seen as a failing.

I was given the name "Alene" so that I could share the Hebrew one of my paternal grandmother, Ethel. I was a specimen without flaw, my health sturdy, if not meeting the definition of pretty. The typical newborn, my face was wrinkly, I having virtually no hair on my supposedly pointy head. That would be the account given, although pictures feature my pleasant, round face with big, dark eyes.

A favorite recollection of my father:

"When the nurse first put you in mum's arms you looked up at me and stuck your tongue out. After immediate shock your mum and I had a good laugh."

My involuntary exhale was an absolute signal of my aliveness. I mean, God forbid, it might have been a clear indication of medical distress. In recounting the intensity of that day, my mother perceived me as offensive, to have no redemption for the purity of my innocence.

CHAPTER 4

I was a buoyant, curious, intuitive infant with my father maintaining *"You didn't cry unduly."* From infancy my training in not creating an embarrassing scene began, when brought to the Sabbath services learning quickly the desire for my silence. In abeyance, my accommodating nature molded. I could have held my mother's ingratiation longer if not for the fact of my learning to talk quite early.

My mother always dressed me up in frilly attire and looking pretty darn girly with a ribbon wrapped around the one strand of hair on my head, I was not fidgety when she walked about with me in my pram. Her story, strange as it sounds, goes that passers-by who caught a glimpse of me would state, *"Oh, what a lovely boy you have!"*

Mark's half brother Ben, together with partner Alan, had purchased a few delightful pieces of nursery furniture, which fit into the beautifully decorated second bedroom. The garden outside included a good stretch of lawn. Most afternoons, weather permitting, my mother set me by her in the pram, we awaiting my father's return from the office. Upon seeing my rosy glee he could not compose himself, delighted by my welcoming joy.

Dolly and Maurice became to me my beloved Nana and Daddy Low. Living close to our apartment, weekends were spent together, they unable to subdue their joy at my presence. My first real memory of Nana was her bending down close to me while my nappy was changed, and with her big smile saying, *"Who's a precious darling?"* Kicking, waving my arms, I shouted back *"me me me me me!"* She adored my reaction, I never tiring of her query.

Full of energy and eager to move about, instead of the average form of crawl, I acquired the art of backstroke crawler by sitting on my bum and pushing backwards with my feet. *Why be like everybody else?* I was improving on my uncustomary arrival, beholding to my individuality. At fifteen months I hit a new bar in diversifying. I walked.

My parents would apparently be in stitches as they were watching me hit the wall, only afterwards turning me around for me to take off again. *Hello, I'm not some toy!*

♥   ♥

By the time of my one-year birthday the decision had been made. My parents and I were going to immigrate to America. In 1957, European life was unchanged from the old-fashioned ideas of generations past, notably the given of family members living within proximity their entire lives. Mark, having enhanced his experiences of independence while living in cosmopolitan London, was enthusiastic of world advancements in technology, his vision not glorified exploration but bringing the quality life not possessed, yet for which he constantly yearned.

America clearly would best serve Mark's furthering his career, and thus, beneficial to the comfort of his family. In telling his in-laws of our leaving they were taken aback. Many discussions in considering the pros and cons were conducted. As he could not let pass the opportunity of his lifetime, everyone appeared unanimous.

♥   ♥

Herbert and Enid were also married by now. They had felt it best to move nearer to Enid's parents in South Wales. Anticipating a spacious environment that favored lots of children and animals, and having the doors always open to company, they found a two-story house that had an expansive backyard—veering from the usual dog and cat variety, raising rabbits no less, to be cared for by their three motivated youngsters, Andrea, Marc and Julian. In the brief English summers, Enid could be found basking in the sun for hours, watching her little ones as they frolicked nearby, tickled by their laughter.

Herbert's career was in optometry and he owned a clinic to which he commuted an hour each way five days a week. For close to half a century he passionately worked his craft, for as long residing in the same merry home.

♥   ♥

Eventually, a long held wish, once revealed, would be brought to fruition.

Nana gave a farewell party with attendees bringing presents for Mark and Rita's dolled up infant who stole the hearts of everyone. The fanciful imagining of their lives in America could not possibly match the realities which were to confront them.

CHAPTER 5

On the landing that afternoon were well-wishers blowing kisses to loved ones gathered along the massive ocean liner's promenade as she readied for her scheduled departure from the Port of Southampton on the south coast of England. The radiance of a blissful sun showing up the British chill, usual formalities discarded, the atmosphere swelled with exuberance, tears requited.

Farewell! ... Bon Voyage!

The third week of November 1957 Mark, Rita, and I were amongst hundreds of courageous passengers to be aboard Her Majesty's RMS *Queen Mary*. Decades earlier the *Titanic* reigned supreme as the largest international luxury vessel manufactured by Great Britain. She touted her safety indisputable, yet subterfuge and corruption would later be determined as hampering the implementations to minimize any loss of life in a perilous event. Differing from her predecessor the *Queen Mary's* irresistibility lay in the privilege of access; not solely catering to those rich and famous, she economical to the general public.

Ten years later she sailed for the last time. Moored permanently at Long Beach harbor in Southern California, she is a fascinating tourist museum listed on the National Registry of Historic Places.

This journey would forever affix our rare connection to Great Britain's maritime history. My father and mother were bent on intertwining the tangible aspects of this heritage as a part of their family dynamic. As for me, this event of grand importance I could not fully grasp, but for the shrill sounds of happiness and fear of a sensorial nature.

♥   ♥

Three years earlier my grandparents were enjoying the blessing of their daughter's marriage. Now, after less than two years with their glorious first grandchild, my parents and I were to be distanced by a traverse of 5,400 miles. With the decision harrowing, Nana and Daddy Low were respectful and would not complicate matters despite their great disappointment.

If my mother had mixed emotions about leaving all the comforts known, she kept her anxiety hidden. She neither wanted her parents nor her husband to feel insecure and doubting. The outcome of this definitive act was reliant on the happiness such an adventure could grant.

"Absence makes the heart grow fonder."

Emotionally torn, the folks received assurance that distance would not matter. My parents would keep their word by arranging alternating visits between England and assisting the folks in coming to see us in the States.

Nana and Daddy Low subsequently followed their son's move to South Wales, settling forty minutes away in the quaint town of Swansea where they could afford a larger house across from Swansea Park, its spacious grounds delighting the relatives who frequented. A few years later moving into an apartment, the first floor of the brownstone held just enough space to set up a darling confectionary shop where they would bestow kindness and generosity as shown in the intimacy of their home to their community at large, merchandising vital goods beyond candy and ice cream.

♥   ♥

Hours passed when finally the *Queen Mary* left the Port at Southampton, first crossing the channel in relative calm to Cherbourg, France where additional passengers would be boarding. The dining room sparkling in formal ornamentation, my parents were led to the specified area serving kosher food, their stomachs grumbling, awaiting not long afterwards a good night's sleep.

The next morning the Trans-Atlantic ship was being met increasingly by rougher weather. Of the three of us, my mother was unable to keep food down or properly rest, for the balance of the trip her experience dreadful.

The constant rocking had not the least bit effect on me or my father, during our strolls I comfortable flowing with the undulation of the ocean's swirls with no handhold.

It was over a week when, in our sites, the Statue of Liberty glowed from New York's Staten Island, my father's breath taken away. America! We three were finally here. My mother sighed in great relief at the ship stilling, our trip terminating at the door of our hotel in Manhattan.

We had long departed the bow of the ship, but my mother's constitution was seriously impaired, she wanting only to stay in bed. My father decided to take me out for a walk—as if honoring our arrival, decorative flags lining the street lamps where thousands gathered in celebrating the timely holiday representing gratitude, Thanksgiving Day.

The boisterous crowd was caught up in the Macy's Parade, excitement bubbling in seeing gigantic balloons, floats, and bands in formation on the several-mile route.

Why did my coming into this world take an eternity when earth is this wonderful!

♥   ♥

It is often lost on parents the messages a child may glean from gestures or facial expressions or by the tone of their words expressed, any of which contain the power of critical manifestation, the adult seemingly unconscious to how their actions, or lack thereof, intuitively resonate with the makeup of the child's self-worth.

My mother's own pride was borne out of emphasis on image, other's perceptions her main focus. I learned to limit beating my own drum, inserting deprecation, tee-ups, before talking about myself because in her opinion such talk showed conceit. Contemptible! Instead of my feeling pleasure when sharing, for example, the unique events of my establishment in the United States, I spoke timorously, a handicap becoming habitual.

CHAPTER 6

In Europe only two denominations of Judaism exist, Orthodox and Reform. Interweaving liturgical teachings to a secular foundation was crucial to my parents. America offered the advantage of the Conservative denomination, in a perfect world a middle ground, being in America not creating any detour from their intent on religious virtue.

My father's secular career aside, he aspired also to the legacy left by his father, to be an esteemed member of the Jewish community for whom he bestowed his fidelity. For my mother, a title of "Cantor's Wife" had a nice ring to it and was what she counted on to cement her profile.

My mother may have thought she was prepared for the complexities of bringing her child up in an increasingly modern society, but no sooner had we set foot in America did the tone of her imputation spark resentment between my parents. My father's destiny was this land of Milk and Honey. The great United States of America beckoned the promise of a nation on the cusp of cutting edge advances and scientific exploration. This more liberal society would heighten self-actualization at light speed.

Their preconceived notion of what correct moralism looked like would be challenged in the years that followed, at times furiously. The cosmopolitan nature of the United States starkly opposed many of the puritanical formalities imbedded in British practice that my parents sanctioned.

♥   ♥

My father's destination was for Southern California, the forefront of the budding aviation industry—for close to forty years employed at CONRAC, Aerojet Rocketdyne, Northrop, Hughes, Bendix and Allied. Our only relatives on this side of the continent were in West Hollywood, my father's half brother Dave, with his wife, Phyllis, and their two boys. They offered our staying with them until my father scoped out a suitable apartment.[4] In nearby Fairfax with its infamous Canter's Delicatessen, he found it on North Vista Drive.

Flying by the seat of his pants he had to believe his search for work in the defense industry would pay off. Out from the dust of atrocities during WWII had come optimal advancements in the field, notably in America.

Money was prioritized leaving frivolous purchases out, the apartment virtually bare. I would prefer to believe I helped my mother, by focusing on me keeping her sanity during what must have felt like unbearable circumstances. I could not know the degree of their struggle. My pleasure was found roaming through our unfurnished surroundings. I had one toy that was hard to nestle up to, but one I could punch, a helium-filled Bozo the Clown. Mostly, my father was my company to the local playground. The jungle gym and slides, I liked it all; oh my favorite, the swings. To this day I will seek out one, riding it as high as I can.

My father's efforts to secure work paid off when he snagged a lucrative post at Hughes Aircraft Corporation in the city of Azusa in the San Gabriel Valley. In those days, the entire area was up and coming with abundant housing construction. Absent the proliferation of strip malls were blocks of flourishing fruit groves.

With his robust tenor pipes, he would find a thriving Conservative membership within the city of West Covina, with its *shul*, Citrus Valley Jewish Temple Center, needing a qualified Cantor. One Sunday during Chanukah a large crowd of married couples with their children was gathered for a picnic, this perfect locality twenty-five miles east of Los

---

4   Their marriage troubled by a string of medical expenditures due to Phyllis' hypochondria, approximately five years later Dave killed her before killing himself. My father was immediately called by Dave's sons asking for help in the aftermath of finding their corpses in the blood-splattered bedroom.

Angeles.[5] A new house was awaiting our entrance. Soon my parents would become fast friends with another couple originally from England who a year earlier had settled with their three daughters in the same town and also belonged. Their closeness would last the whole of their lives.

Coming into a real sense of my separate self, I was stimulated by an era refreshed.

---

5   This *shul* united with another and it is now named Temple Ami Shalom.

CHAPTER 7

I was growing fast, offering my mother many more opportunities at dressing me like a doll. She had a terrific eye, a million dollar want-to-be without the exorbitant bite from my father's pocketbook. This was her comfort zone, buying clothes, feeling it an expression of love toward me while she the recipient of compliments.

♥ ♥

An expectant mother tends towards imagining, out of proportion, a magical arrival. My mother wanted to not spoil the surprise so she had no hint of my sex, although once here her ideas left barely room for distinguishing her child's identity from her own.

Encapsulating a carefree, energetic spirit, I innately was inquisitive, perceptive and analytical, I understanding plenty before I could talk. I relished my fascination on all I saw. As my field of vision expanded in my transformative years, my mother's every nuance seemed to illuminate to me the gap of misunderstanding between us. Indicative of expert Piaget's child developmental charting, I showed excellence in processing information and conceptualizing, progressing through myriad stages, without concerns. A normal child, I wanted to jump and run and get a bit dirty.

Research emphasizes the harm of an overly symbiotic connection between a mother and daughter—the ties that bind less unconditional but consistent control effectuating emotional incest. Once enabled with speech I felt a wave of fear and anxiety trapping her, motivating every reaction.

A raw love, I felt my mother protective, as strongly, the pull of my identity pre-destined.

♥   ♥

"Who do you think you are, the Queen of Sheba?"

This just one of the numerous remarks my mother was disposed to exclaim towards me. With her concerted effort being assurance of my not getting *"a big head,"* she acted as the faultfinder, discounting rather than praising.

How could she see this strategy as building a confident personality?

My mother's carriage was frankly fanciful, laced in vanity. Her ego exuded that of royalty as her presumption was the recipient of loyal acquiescence. I rationalized her present concept of the world as a skewed perception, but my life would be spent struggling to fix her patterned stance.

♥   ♥

My mother often remarked contemptuously, *"You're so much like your father."* I am grateful.

Not competing for his attention, I would be nowhere without it. I had already gleaned my mother's discounting me rather than providing validation, my father having to make up for her lack of attachment.

Lean but muscular my handsome father wore his virility, his thick head of hair proportionate to that about his chest, favoring European beach attire in briefs unabashedly. A proponent of athleticism he knew the empowering lesson of discipline.

It was impossible to satisfy my mother, her disposition depressive. She was not able to get a handle on her damaging behaviors. Her weaknesses overwhelmed the beauty of experience, she begrudging the quotient of compatibility between me and my father.

My mother understood her role as satisfying basic necessities—a roof over my head, clothes, enough food to eat—but impression focused, my just being a child did not equate to acceptance of unbecoming childlike behaviors, her stern quashing to eliminate embarrassment. I craved her affection, not the isolation of an undesirable.

I understood that abeyance might put me in a good light, but I could not escape my mother's glare expressing a strong disapproval, my long-lasting mental snapshots of her disagreeable. I instinctually knew her comportment to be foreign to my person. She mistrusted the depth of my love. She met my growing up and my having my dreams with resistance. There was no middle ground, her attitude my conforming or accepting her wounding rejection.

Had I been showered with her smiles and cuddles that demonstrative warmth would linger as my recollection. In fact, my development from infant to toddler, bringing with it verbal communications of specific wants and dislikes, only made for her articulated opinion; I was unruly. She projected displeasure upon my attempts to learn independence, choosing an emotional distancing, rather than to validate. Then she would scold, "*You're not an affectionate child,*" as another objection.

In real time, I was her reflection, living all that I was learning. I could no more bestow affection upon her when I felt her condemnation of natural behaviors. Her attitude towards sheer playfulness, joy for the simple sake of joy, was impatience if not intolerance. Her ruling emotion was the big "W", excessively worrying to irrational extremes to the point of overprotection. The definitive good mother is what she believed; this felt more dangerous than bruising my knees on the playground. I needed her attitude to be calming, not always on edge.

Could I only anticipate her nurturing in response to trouble?

Not remiss in gifting attention my father was eager for opportunities to walk with me, help me learn, read to me the classics of nursery rhymes, Dr. Seuss, and Aesop's Fables. In all probability, my mother believed she was being considerate in giving him this time.

Why was she more inclined to stay behind? What about her quality time with me? Couldn't she switch from the rigid, possessive mother to a fonder interacting?

She could not.

♥   ♥

My story's origin, it is important to note, is rooted in the experiential, as greatly as the factual. It speaks to the rivaling maternal influence—a subjective assessment of my emotional stages prompting automatic criticism—that negative reinforcement in the child psyche. The absolute determinant to one's successful life course exists solely in the conditioning of the child's emotional wellness.

In God's infinite majesty, I came into the world with the power and individualism that all babies are bestowed. In spite of my strongest start my destined happiness relied more on nurture. My mother desiring nothing but my best, I was learning how my painstaking efforts in gaining her satisfaction did not square with my personal happiness.

I am not educated in the science of astrology, but I am of the belief that parents should be aware that a sign's personality characteristics hold a valuable key to a child's distinctive traits. To discredit this inherency of personality, formed by the alignment of the planets at that child's birth in the natural world, hinders the parent's full appreciation of their child's uniqueness.

Nana and Daddy Low's birthdays fell, respectively, on the first and second day of July, Nana his junior. Both Gemini, their legend: mutable under a same ruling planet; on a similar wave length their relationship infused with the mutual set of qualities.

As for a sign's elemental force, if a sun sign's energy is not identical, it is helpful to have the compatible link between traits and quirks in serving united efforts—air relating to water; water's relationship to earth tricky due to the destructive capacity. Further is the possibility of fire's havoc upon earth.

Thus, my mother's internalized framework relative to Dolly—air to earth—made their relationship well suited, she amenable to her mother's expectations and discipline, rather than experiencing feelings of enforced domination. Nana and Maurice saw their daughter's essence as good, which allowed some freedom for my mother just to be....

♥   ♥

I wish I could say that a comparable understanding existed between me and my mother. She saw, only, I was not the absolute carbon copy for whom she had intensely hoped, and she would not completely get past that reality. She deemed my character's traits and talents threatening based on their looking different. Here, the family dynamic overpowers energy forces. Both of my parents share the earth sign of Virgo, yet my father easily accepted my fiery Aries nature. He got me!

Little girl wonder....

CHAPTER 8

The enemy discourages dreams.
My hope for a sincerely positive connection with my mother was to soon be breached, for by the time we moved into our first house on Meadow Road she was showing. A few months shy of three, I was proceeding to define me. *How big a splash can I make in this pool called Life?*

I have but two memories of that period. My mother gave me a beautiful doll the size of a real baby, and with it a wood-slatted cot and outfits. Her face aglow, I gave her the name "Lilly," and I was her mommy. A tremendously happy occasion came when I received the precious gift of an olive-eyed pure black kitten. Tender in disposition, this may have been a deciding factor in my not carrying in my nature superstitious tendencies. I instinctively held great love for animals, and like the family in Africa who become caretakers of wild lions in the wonderful nature epic *Born Free*, I caressed the fantasy of a menagerie consisting of a lion cub, bear cub or even a chimpanzee. As that was out of the question, "Tibby" as he would be known, would suffice as my first real friend. He took to me immediately, he a surrogate for attention with my mother's elsewhere. I adored him throughout his eighteen years of life.

♥   ♥

Changes were near with the approaching birth. My parents had the preference of wanting a boy; I but looking forward to being the oldest, that mattering, someone upon whom this new person could depend.

During the last couple of months of her pregnancy, my mother was diagnosed with a hyperthyroid condition, likely brought on by stressors such as the unlikelihood of a natural birth due to similar complicating factors present at my birthing. Based on this prognosis, she was given a choice of two treatments: have her thyroid removed, or be given a round of radioactive iodine.

Psychologically pressured, she accepted the latter option. Her personal appearance ruling, she did not want the minutest scar on her neck. Common sense aside, not the least of which, the physician surely availed of potential serious harm to the fetus—"*radioactive*," the term inferring danger—a huge red flag setting off no alarm bells. Vanity outweighed possible repercussions, her judgmental lapse to haunt, forever.

My mother once again was forced to undergo another C-section. She had hoped of perhaps having one more child, but the doctors made no bones about the fact of an increased danger to her own life should she become pregnant again, another surgery inevitable. No doubt, for my mother the receipt of this information was just another in a chain of unfortunate outcomes that only increased her irrationality of perceived injustice.

On May 18, 1959 my brother Warren came into the world, and with his arrival their brief disappointment at the news they would have no more children quickly subsided. In spite of their trepidation, their saved memory of his birth would be jubilance as they tightly held their cherub-faced, healthy, beautiful baby boy, now the family balanced.

My parents waited until I turned the big three, in the belief of my instantly adjusting to the newborn's demands. Naturally fascinated by this new presence I could watch him in his crib. A way to be helpful I thought was entertaining myself for there would be many chances for talking and playing with my buddy.

Besides reading, I found a love for classical music as my father's favorite passion was having the melodious sounds about the house. Who could not appreciate such immense glory by myriad composers' everlasting masterful contributions? The exposure was influential, it uplifted when I was lonely, a gravitational escape. Over the years my musical tastes were to grow eclectic, kindling my desire to make a career in the industry as a singer.

♥   ♥

The pang of emotional detachment I clearly sensed from my mother moved beyond the temporary. Her ways were set as were her expectations from me, still a child in my own right. Perhaps another's adjustment might have been easier to flow with the turn of events; I not so able. I required attention, not in excess, but enough to satisfy my ordinary sensitivities. I expected my mother would notice; instead, she tossing aside my needs as exaggerated.

"*You're overly sensitive.*" I believed my feelings to be significant, but what I felt was non-acceptance, as if in the way somehow, feeling any closeness between me and her slipping from my grasp. She transferred her abundant focus onto her son while, simultaneously, more emotional responsibility onto my toddler shoulders.

I sensed some definite inequality. It was not something imagined. It was wrong, I was sure, yet alone I was in my thoughts, my feelings, in emotional turmoil. It must be me I subconsciously believed. I must do all in my power to be perfect, to do and be exactly as she wished. Then I would feel her whole love.

The word "should" was imprinted as a precursor to instructing. Of course, I felt honor towards my parents. I looked up to them, I believed they held every answer, they adults, purposeful and correct in all matters of critique.

I put my father on a pedestal for his intelligence, his common sense approach to life. Because he was away in the daytime occupied at his employment, his beliefs about the inner workings of the household in his absence fell far short of the reality.

My mother's ailments not immensely debilitating—hyperthyroidism, a bout of Bell's palsy and hypertension—she found them useful when manipulating an outcome, as characteristic of emotional codependency on my father.

I believe she suffered also from depression but she dared not divulge any emotional struggles, their existence a fabrication of the mind, my father alone assigned as the accomplice in her masquerade.

To the congregants our family seemed the epitome of a close-knit bond.

A paradigm shift was already brewing inside of me. I was not going to change anymore than my mother could change. When noticing me she expressed meanness and judgment, her ills shaping her as an insecure woman who bullies in false promotion of being sturdy.

Her duty was to provide guidance to me, not simply authority. The same sex parent meant her influence to be the greatest in my life. Surely, deep in her heart she knew she had the power to be more available to me, giving me the tools to build my self-esteem. I was a child, older than my brother by only three years, and still longing to feel the extent of her loving. Yet, my mother's responding was not in accord with the recognition of my needs. I had become her property, obligated to her impulses which, I felt, often defied practicality. She was impossible to reach, yet she was attributing my nature as causing her incapacitation.

It felt like I was being groomed as her caretaker, a non-beneficial, unnatural interdependence stemming from frenzied emotion. Following the protocol my grandparents had handed down, the standard belief remained: *"Children should be seen, but not heard."* I did not have to be old to know the inherent issue of oppression under this mantra; it would never jive with me. Being a child was not going to make inconsequential my thoughts and feelings.

I needed my mother, but her insensitivity felt like an unshakable loss, her emotional abandonment cutting to my soul's core. I loved my new brother deeply, without jealousy; this was not about him at all. It was one thing to be taking care of my cat and quite another feeling I was not being fully validated.

Why was my presence seemingly the cause for her ambivalence?

When she called, when she needed me to help her, or had instructions about something, I came running, that seemingly the extent of her attention; the obsessive worry and over-control motivations keeping me in my place, she staying top cat with reprimands and belittling. As no one else was around to see that her parenting was less than reaffirming, she was free in effectuating harm absent any adversaries.

To not grow up surrounded by the adoration of my grandparents, and other dear relatives, gravely impressed upon my lonely world.

I was open, interested in the deeper meaning of life and why I was here.

My mother had very strong opinions about her role in my life and although she may have taken some advice from the expert Dr. Spock, her go-to was to elicit righteous intimidation when disagreeing, believing this condoned by God. All respect was due to her, deeming it unnecessary to return the same favor back to me.

♥   ♥

Outwardly, I pretended as if I was happy, but in my psyche feeling a clear opposition, my mother undermining my every move, any decisions made having immensely more to do with how she would feel and be portrayed, and absent consideration of the affects on me. "*My ways*"—insulting my normal nature—when evidenced, did not appear pleasant to her, leaving me feeling an ever more forceful longing for my personal imprint.

In summing up my fourth and fifth years this internal disturbance only kept building, like a crushing of my spirit. I became increasingly introspective, throughout these two years trying to figure out how to effectively verbalize what I was feeling. I proceeded well in school but at home I felt like staying as scarce as possible.

In between other duties I finished my homework. I felt pride to some extent, having accomplished a lot by this age, at other times feeling less than comforted by the lack of natural conversation between my mother and me. She was there protecting and sheltering me from the ugly world, yet her posture was cold.

She could not seem to control her emotionality nor attempt much self-correction. She reinforced her teaching about the hard knocks, life being unfair, and specifically, my wants of little significance. She could not see how she was exaggerating fears about inherent dangers, a bubble wrapping of great hindrance.

My interest in the knowing was huge, that nature of a child craving knowledge of the good and bad and everything in between the universe offers. My mother felt it was best to shield me, imagining harm through an understanding of life, a manifestation of fear forming an intention to incorrect guidance which I would only realize much later. My experience of the world was confused, at once dreamy and idealistic, contrasted by the roots of unsettlement.

Books about child development confirm how one's sense of identity is formed by the age of three. My mother wanted children desperately but was critically unprepared for the immensity of raising a healthy and happy person. Her life had been relatively uncomplicated before Warren and I came along.

As consistent as was my father's support, her ease seemed dependent upon his literally being at her side. When not physically present, my mother felt overwhelmed. Her insecurities boded ominous for normal interactions as we grew up.

In spite of the wonderful life my father was doing all in his power to provide, my mother often laid accusations at his feet, blasting his efforts. His success allowed many opportunities from which my mother reaped the benefits. Yet, her assumption was everyone else's lives possessing more reasons for feeling that happy perfection.

Her lack of self-assuredness belied her upbringing and present situation. How convenient to convey bitterness and discontent in the face of the riches given her. Unable to be happy hampered an authentic expression of joy. My father saw evidence, but the truth would stay in darkness. He had not realized his role to be an enabler, but the life he envisioned was fast becoming a shrill obscurity; he not living his life anymore but the course set by my mother.

♥   ♥

It was imperative we looking the part when holding center stage. My mother and her attractive husband were the welcoming fit to an increase in the *shul* membership to capacity and, as if my father's plate was not full enough, he assumed another leadership as chairman of the board.

One of his many duties as Cantor was teaching the up-and-coming Bar Mitzvah boys and Bat Mitzvah girls all of the required prayers and Torah portions specific to their Hebrew birthdates, while at the pulpit he charged with the engaging of the congregation in song along with his choir.

I discovered my singing voice as a toddler; genetic unquestionably, indeed, I with the making of a songstress. Harmonizing came easily to me, as did the ability to read music, my body absorbing its euphoria.

My mother's voice was sweet, and Warren's tuneful, my father beaming with pride to see all of us each time he turned to start us up in chorus. The families attending services were full of admiration for our improving the *shul* experience, their courteous smiles and respect seemingly indicating their envy at our prime example.

Our private reality a far cry from how we appeared, I struggled with the notion we were putting on airs, phony, spiting ourselves at the expense of satisfying our public.

My mother had no problem with our deception, but it felt completely counter-intuitive to my development. My heart's intent was practicing honesty, being real, kind and loving to all of God's creatures; I without choice burdened with discomfort and placing into question my own rational thinking.

While portraying herself as having been forced into leaving England, forsaking her parents and relatives, it is my belief that my mother desired escaping the small town existence, while anticipative of her offspring doting on her for her complete fulfillment.

Sadly for my father, a few years into life in America my mother did not hesitate to verbalize her dislike at being in this country, basing perceived problems and misfortune as the fault of his bringing her here. By now, my father's realization of his testimonial for his greatest love required her needs being consequential beyond his. He swallowed her resentment, fending off hurt, convinced she would get over it.

♥   ♥

I was human. I felt everything...all that my mother felt I felt. My mother did not understand the impact of her parental style, resembling more the Victorian era and not the Age of Aquarius. She was accustomed to being the receiver of caring, of others helping to feed her self-worth and ego.

Her brief teaching of children in Jewish day school was no preparation for raising her own. In that brand new territory I was her first experiment. *Where could I go from here?*

CHAPTER 9

Had I been born a male, all would likely have been different. It was acceptable to allow boys to be boys, free to explore their fullest potential. Warren, from the moment she saw him, was the apple of her eye, she in the palm of his hand. I had no chance of competing ever with that.

My mother believed his personality to be so similar to hers, which had no basis in fact. She had to maneuver a counter-promotion of their tightness against me and my father, Warren's wants and needs not met with harshness but happiness, warmth, love, unconditionally.

My mother planned a party for my sixth birthday. I was very excited and was enjoying the event with a bunch of friends. That is, until my mother walked out with a cake and put it in front of Warren seated at the head of the table. As all eyes diverted to him, I wanted to yell *this is my birthday, not his!*

♥   ♥

My clarity sharpened once I turned six. I was suffering a trauma, an emotional desertion the likes of which I knew undeserved. I felt my mother did not love me. Her tunnel vision conservatism confined my gender and together with religious obligations created constant friction. I needed to elevate my personal beliefs in order to improve my sense of my development not being disrupted.

When I attempted to express myself in any fashion, I was met with my mother's reactive, subjective projection: I was being overly dramatic, too sensitive and, oh, selfish! She faulted me, proclaiming I was difficult and impossible to understand, this her common retort.

With her watery gaze, she with my father's backup, served up this reminder statement: *"We love you and only want what's best for you."*

That would be all well and good, if not for the sheer manipulative falsehood. They were making single-handed determinations for my life while deeming it unnecessary to heed critical listening. Expressing upset, their perception I impertinent, followed by their reiteration to my well-being at their heart.

Childhood is not all fun and games but serious at times. The trials and tribulations of social fitness, the expectations of parents, teachers; like a spirited bunny bounding across a sun-flowered field oblivious to its ineptitude in dodging the giant ready to pounce on its jubilance.

At six, my emotional framework basically solidified, my journey of discovery had begun in quest of the deeper focus on my future personal growth. I knew I was rational, a sensible girl, my sole motivation, being recognized.

This is my life; I'm going to make my loving parents know if I'm unhappy.

My exhausted father often barely had his foot in the door before being barraged by my mother's interpretation about her day and my disruptive behavior. Trusting the information received, the story condemning, I awaited his approach to my bedroom, anxious for the chance to tell him what really happened.

I was on defense, a perpetual antagonist, my explanation inconsequential; accepting her version my father stating *"I think you should apologize for upsetting your mother."*

I was overruled, accused and sentenced.

♥   ♥

From the time Warren was about three my mother presumed I would look out for him and I wanted nothing more than to further express my compassionate side. Although I was playful, he was a handful. He preferred teasing me or picking on me unabashedly, I not taking easily to such feistiness and searching out my mother to make him stop. She believed it my duty to handle the ruckus: *"You're the oldest; I don't want to know about it.*" Trying to flex my communication skills—rehearsing the words in my head from fear of her incorrect receipt of them—I was virtually ineffective in a personally beneficial result.

In every situation she had to be right, so therefore I must be in the wrong.

It felt as though I was absent, my mother's arbitrary judgment was discounting what I was saying as if nonsense. The more I tried standing up for myself the more she slammed me down. She had apparently skimmed over what has been purported by psychologists, while concurring in the child's resilience. This truth, however, only exists when the child is removed from a toxic environment and placed in a more embracing one.

"*The world does not revolve around you,*" she in my face, this message received loud and clear, assuring that I was beneath her. In her twisted frame, the world revolved around her. The truth, she dominated her universe. "*You think you're so hard done by,*" intimated irrelevance of any dissatisfaction in my hemisphere. She proclaimed I was sick, with accusations that I was being unkindly jealous of her affections toward my brother.

Did I not have the right to the same support?

♥   ♥

My parents shaded messages in subtext, nuanced by a double standard, with the banality of platitudes and discretionary inaccuracy fueling my vexation. *Which way was really up?* They did not like seeing me moping; I usually kept close my tears; I smiled big in pictures; when pictured with me, my mother's visible lack of joy proving our detachment.

Child psychology and behavioral science has taken quantum leaps, the humanities—the branches of learning concerned with human thought within the framework of interpersonal relations—motivating shifts in the advancing of parental education as it pertains to the cognitive and emotional development of children. Throughout the ages, lest we forget, bold parenting skills evolved through their simple willingness to put first their children's needs in that moment before any revisiting of forbearer traditions. This approach did not depend on formal education as much as basic common sense of it the best guarantee of raising a self-assured child.

Trendsetters were stepping up their theories of less dissection, the sensible accented, logical ideas of a baby boomer generation urging to make obsolete prejudice and oppression, forcibly opening minds in grand affirmation of deserved societal freedoms and equality for women and, in turn, a tutorial structure enhancing the best from a child. This groundwork, set in the Twentieth Century, offered up better rules for the advancement of an individual's future achievements in all aspects of life.

On a segment of *The Today Show* years ago a child development expert was speaking on eight critical lessons parents should implement by a child's fifth year. Initially, the result of teaching assertiveness is self-validation and assuredness. In fact, a child's self-confidence will help in deterring traits and behaviors usually evidenced by a child who feels their worthiness is undermined. In other words, confidence is not the recipe in forming a huge ego; rather egotism is spawned through the lack thereof.

My parents were stuck in a time warp, all they had been accustomed to believing as correct and acceptable met with questioning, upon my persona a disproportionate subdual.

♥   ♥

I discovered my sexual reality in my sixth year, the ecstasy of personal exploration, however brief, would beg on my brain as a fantastical urge to be regularly repeated.

It was my mother's idea, I taking ballet, at Elizabeth Baird Dance Studio. She believed this form of exercise to be best for achieving a healthy posture. I was flourishing, gaining a dancer's graceful artistry, the music stimulating. I loved learning the routines from the famous ballets and, decked out in gorgeous costumes, receiving opportunities for audience performances. I so delighted in being on the stage, in the appreciation, validation, as an addict wanting more.

In first grade I quickly demonstrated my smarts and sailed through. My parents, however, threw a wrench into my going forward when they told me they believed it best to keep me back—repeating first grade for my advancing with kids my age—I have to assume my mother was the culprit.

How puzzling; rather than cultivate the intelligence I was evidencing, lowering my credibility, while fanning the over concern of a one-year age differential!

♥   ♥

A mother's unwavering support is the driving force in her child's success, unequivocally if a same sex child.

My mother feared my knowing, not welcoming my inquisitiveness, her stance confrontational and inflexible to adjustments as contrary to reasoning. I had felt this at three; it was now most evident.

The commercial for L'Oréal originally used the tagline, "because I'm worth it" but my mother, hearing this, thought it disgusting. In figuring her belief of similar encouragement as harmful, I can only conclude that need was her scale in calculating love and that I must be kept doubting, dependent on her influence.

Seeing a woman flaunt her looks was sluttish in my mother's opinion, yet in the same breath she put immense importance on her impeccable appearance—drawing in a beauty spot between her eyes for exoticism to replicate the look of Elizabeth Taylor.

Assertive, confident, worthy are the traits expected of a mother to embolden in her daughter, not deem them improper. Surely, I deserved the same rights to flattery, of which all girls espouse, yet such notions were not suitable according to my mother, a startling reactionary wallop her exhibition.

♥   ♥

Emotional and mental problems seemed to be impeding my mother's incapacity to relate to me; my father's choice was dispelling my feelings. However counter-intuitive, he was at the mercy of my mother's capricious qualities. He inserting momentary humor, I was feeling a constant fight for absolution. *What on earth was happening here?*

My mother could not bring herself to acknowledge her limitations any more than give credibility to me, it easier to stifle my expression altogether. She did not realize the costly impact causing our relationship into deterioration. It was not my fault, God knows!

At six, I was consumed by feelings of defeat in the midst of my current emotionality. My heart was crushed under this fog of sadness and I felt completely helpless in knowing how on earth to deal, or not deal, with everything being so insanely wrong. Inconsolably crying in bed one night I wanted this hellish descent over, thinking it better if I was gone. I could not stand feeling this way. Maybe my mother was right.

Maybe there's something seriously wrong with me.

Internally, I heard what I believed to be the voice of God. With my pain calming, my horrid thoughts silencing, my feelings of mistreatment were assuaged, the message a confirmation of blessed perfection simply the way I am.

My spiritual connection with the magnificence of a higher power I would not doubt even when tested, it my constant source of reliability through my darkest times.

♥   ♥

Hypocrisy seemed in plain sight, from my family and many in the congregation, a lie hidden in their belief that they were more deserving of God's goodness due to their devoted ritualism. I was smart enough to know there was no fooling The Almighty. Regardless of the innumerable years I would be force-fed religious practice, the truth was always there that humanity's essential directive is sincerity spread through loving words and deeds.

CHAPTER 10

Existing in the dichotomous zone of moxie and fear of not having the tough constitution to reap life's eventual rewards, I got that it was all on me in getting there.

♥   ♥

I was attaining a greater understanding of my faith. *"Do unto others as you would have them do unto you."*

My father reflected often on one aspect of Judaism. Inherent in the Talmud's teachings is the emphasis on the bending with the times, it crucial that religious practice not exclude the secular enhancements for the fullest quality of life. In his mind the distinction, his actions were molded at the mercy of my mother's blurred lines; she the woman of the house and in charge. Absent an ease in her presence she meted out pre-Shabbat chores with the formality of a drill sergeant and when I did not jump with the appropriate enthusiasm, I insubordinate: *"You little whippersnapper!"*

I did my best, spending hours cleaning silver items, I vacuumed, I helped in the kitchen...I feared her rebuke, my efforts invariably less than perfect.

My mother was a fantastic cook. She loved spending time perfecting recipes carried down from her mother; however, the kitchen was not my favorite place to be. Naturally, my lacking interest in the aspiration caused her displeasure. She mocked me, claiming without these proper skills no man would want to marry me. No amount of compliance could deter her angst.

The whole family was in attendance at every Friday night and Shabbat morning service, usually atop the pulpit with my father as part of the choir. I had been exhibiting a well-toned soprano voice, earning me chances of solos as well as duets with my father.

♥   ♥

Ms. Baird had been so pleased with my excelling in dance for six years. When my mother came to pick me up one day, she pointedly called us over to compliment me. My mother's interests were elsewhere, having initiated my attendance at Hebrew High School and preparing for my Bat Mitzvah.

Sitting in the backseat on the drive home, from out of nowhere, my mother informed me that I would not be returning to ballet class. A highlight of my life, it had filled my heart's emptiness. My father enabled the experience of watching live world renowned dancers Margot Fonteyn, Mikhail Baryshnikov, and Rudolf Nureyev in *The Sleeping Beauty, Cinderella, The Nutcracker, Swan Lake*...I, for a long time, seriously picturing myself in the profession of a ballerina. Granted, it might have been a ridiculous dream, but it was mine!

My mother knew of its great importance, none of that mattering, unbelievably, this unilateral decision void of any discussion. A torpedo rendering me breathless, my heart tattered, I deserved some say. I was twelve!

She leaned towards her other child, whom she saw as less outwardly confrontational, for gratitude indulgence. *"Like chalk and cheese;"* she sought out Warren. He was her palatable choice. Towards me her actions were toxic. With other events similarly defining, the result would be a lifelong search for survival, on my terms.

Chronic depression set in during my adolescence; my parents did not see it obligatory to either recognize or alter their actions. My father was drawn into nights of sparring, my mother in a rare instance pushing him to the brink, losing control, a physical attack. In extreme remorse, she would keep her promise to never let him forget the pain she instigated.

My father's temperance not calming her animosity, she accused him and me of ganging up on her. He gave in to her law—she was right, always—against the brick wall, I alone to certify my sanity.

My father was a leader who promoted the ideals gluing mankind together. He was loved by everyone. He was graciously giving of his time and attention at a moment's notice to those in need. Yet, blind he was with his devotion to my mother, his loyalty dwarfed by weakness; my mother knowing exactly what buttons to push his relenting, in the home she the victor.

Placating to her, he held a conviction of having love enough for the two of them.

♥   ♥

I would not succumb to such hurtful belittling. I told myself I would not be damaged, that I was strong enough to let it all roll off my shoulders. I internalized the cutting, I subconsciously buying all of it. If my own mother felt this way about me then it must be true. I did not deserve to be loved; I did not deserve to be happy.

Such distasteful feelings don't truly get erased from the mind, only outwardly camouflaged.

My life, whet in possibility, I wanted to soar, to keep dreaming big, I invincible.

I was expected to be all smiles in other's company, even to people clearly disingenuous. It was imperative for me not to put on acts, but shy, many of my peers, notably those in the congregation, concluded I was a snob, totally off target. Still, I was often alone feeling sad and helpless.

I sought out professional advice in self-help books, extracting some satisfaction for my internal doubting. My father's study contained a collection of material on eclectic subjects, psychology one, exhausting those books before purchasing new ones, in need of expert objectivity.

My acute sensitivity—my preferred definition—made me more receptive to how other people were thinking and feeling. I wholeheartedly trusted my capacity for listening, to the extent that acquaintances would sometimes reach out to me when they were troubled. My mother was better able in her show of compassion to some dog on the street than to me.

Now I realize animals have no conscience to decide right from wrong or good from evil. Yet, they are trusting, understanding love when they get it, knowing abuse if they receive that. As for what they alone give, they need not think about it.

♥   ♥

"You're nothing but trouble. I'll make you sorry you were ever born."

Punishment usually consisted of spanking, or going to bed without dinner. I cannot forget one day, my mother irate at my supposedly talking back. As my father was not present to stop her, she washed my mouth with soap—in defense of my mother's feelings, I recall another instance at eighteen, my father storming my room and slapping me across the face—it was clear, I not being allowed similar latitude to that of my peers. It seemed like I was living on another planet. I had adopted an inferiority complex, even questioning my being born at the wrong time.

"Be careful not to upset your mother," I would hear regularly from my father. My mere legitimacy of rightfully deserving to communicate and receive any approval from my mother was, in fact, qualified based on how she might be affected. I could barely spit the words out of my mouth before receiving her histrionic attacks.

The older I got, my anxiety and trepidation became increasingly disruptive. With no official diagnosis I believe the impactful experiences delivered through my mother's negativity during my development had the effectuation of post-traumatic stress. She pointedly drew comparisons to my friends, the very few counted on one hand, inquiring of me *"Why can't you be more like them?"*

My standard-bearer by whom I measured impression, she spurned me while conveying praise on peers of whom she had no real knowledge, she clueless that she was hurting me. Like second nature, my mother had to make certain I knew I did not merit equally.

CHAPTER 11

Lively conversations usually took place around the dinner table. I was impassionate on such topics as human rights, I expounding with my father comfortably on the ugliness of political controversy in hampering life—in particular, the Vietnam War and the futility of the United States' involvement, presidents over the course of twenty years insanely believing it the correct approach in spite of the hundreds of thousands of treasured men and women of my generation having their lives snuffed out—also, the centuries-old racist oppression on people of color, first the enslavement in America of four million, to the two-decade Apartheid in South Africa, as their historical experience of intolerance is a similar collective of our Jewish ancestry. The only species of animal with an existential proclivity for brutality, man.

A calming visionary, my father seeing the glass half full theorized on the future of mankind's survival as reliant upon the universal vesting in equality for the sustenance of civilization.

♥   ♥

A few years earlier our parents decided it was time to move to a larger house, the backyard facilitating guests while allowing exercise room for two dogs: "Willie," a collie and shepherd mix, and "Ruben," a Chihuahua mutt. They provided an immensity of comfort unlike any person.

We walked through a block or two of orange groves to get to our individual schools. I was learning a majority of subjects, getting above average scores in homework and tests. Mathematics was an exception, beyond the elementary understanding some stumbling.

Such expertise tied in with my father's profession, I needed his help in comprehending algebraic and geometric concepts. *"You just need to apply yourself"* was easy for him to say, but did not help. His aptitude overwhelming his patience, when I asked for a less complex explanation for problem solving the result was further frustration, my experience a reinforcement of my inadequacy.

Our family's income level was middle class but one would be hard pressed to recognize that from my mother's wanting. In order for my breadwinning father looking up to snuff, he wore suits personally tailored. He was losing his hair in his prime, a stigmatic image my mother would not expose. He bore the expense of a toupee to please her, in public wearing that rug for the remainder of his life.

♥   ♥

He did not see himself as an outdoorsman, and for my mother that was fine, she with an aversion to camping, or hiking, and forget about skiing. Still, my father did take me and Warren up to Mt. Baldy to play in the snow. Such a memorable day, throwing snowballs and having the time of our lives, the excursion a onetime experience.

My mother, unsurprisingly, snubbed playing sports as ridiculous for a girl.

She did not interrupt Warren's interest and need for involvement in any sports. Be it his favorite, basketball, or table tennis, bike riding, or marbles, he was a regular Joe, patriotically endorsing all things American. He had also in me a formidable competitor since I similarly enjoyed these activities as a means of relating to him.

Warren tended to conceal his real feelings for me. We could seem so close, and then irritating each other, he acting bullish, as a Taurus does, and I rallying my ram. At the end of the day, in spite of our distinct personalities, he liked the person I was and he appreciated the challenges I brought.

We had a regular babysitter pleasing to my mother, her qualifications giving peace of mind when our parents went on date nights. Her name escapes me, but not her eccentricity which we detected while spending time together. Liking her and her outrageous interests we looked forward to our parents leaving. She was fanatical about roller derby, watching tough women battling it out in the rink on television, hilarity balancing its violent intensity. Afforded this glimpse into her persona, Warren and I got a kick out of it, unrestricted.

What our mother didn't know couldn't hurt her.

♥   ♥

My father might have lost, too young, the support of his loving parents, yet a spirited portrait was emboldened, his abundant sweetness instilled with humor, propelling an acceptance. He lived by a guiding trust within and less in leaning on approval. From his makeup, he could never be intentionally hurtful, his gift of manifesting goodness and harmony his driving principles.

The one day designated for family fun was Sunday, to a symphony concert or a movie, with my mother's mood uplifting. Musical films a staple, I became enamored with the superstars of the day, notably Barbra Streisand, my idol. They exposed me to spoonfuls of romanticism, the handsome prince with me his soul mate, somewhere out there enormous love and a happily ever after!

To dine out was par for the course for ending Sunday's outing. My mother rationalized strictly Kosher in the home need not restrict her from a day off cooking and the luxury of a nice meal in a pleasurable eatery. Relieved to be out of the house, our lightened energy bubbled into an uproarious laughter at my father's knack for one-liners the likes of the famous Catskill comedians.

The paradox in this weekly excursion is not wasted on those critical elements of *kashrut*, its origins not relying simply on clean plates and non-meat products comprising the delectable food; but as we were not, in the true sense, Orthodox, the conduct could be enforced while having the best of culinary adventures.

♥   ♥

Envisioning an artistic profession in musical theatre was, in my mother's opinion, an unsavory contemplation for a *"nice Jewish girl."* It would not be difficult guessing the complications ahead, I refusing this outrageous ploy. Not only would I dream of it, but duly recognizable the support of others towards my undeniable talents. I could possibly attain notoriety, at all cost I pursuing this goal.

My mother attempted sabotage that fueled mutual resentment while what fed my vigor was my father's show of encouragement. Her modus operandi for my entire life was supplied in the formation of emotional strangulation. She preferred keeping me small, under her wing and less prepared for playing the game of life so as to stay honoring her commands. A serious-minded young lady, I felt unequipped with the knowledge of winning from the fruits of my efforts.

A necessary piece of furniture to finish off her living room—its gorgeous décor reserved only for the pleasure of entertaining visitors— was a piano. My mother's idea was not to be generous to her musically inclined daughter with the chance at learning accompaniment for herself, but having Warren tutored, his lessons brief since he was into guitar.

I decided I wanted to have formal singing lessons. Next to the *shul* choir, opera trumped a sleazy image of a common stage act. My mother's skewed thought process reverberating as static in my mind, a constant interrupting.

♥   ♥

Entering my first of three years of middle school in 1968 brought on fresh anxiety, the desperate pressure of wanting to make new friends, to find acceptance. A great start would have been my mother accepting the change in time. Girls my age were wearing makeup, stockings; she was not adhering to any allowance of my right to passage despite my Bat Mitzvah being the invitation for witnessing my maturity to womanhood. Professing to not be a prude, she wanted me staying childlike, disallowing insights into beautifying my young body in the context of its virtue.

As with a lot of adults, it was the idiotic belief of my mother that educating was basically direction for practice. My father took charge of providing me a facts of life book. For crying out loud, I was a flower child, of that generation catapulted into the erogenous orbit. Any discussion about sex or money my mother decided was unacceptable.

Even popular music increasingly euphemized sexuality. A song from a favorite band, Bread, had this line: *"I want to make it with you,"* its slight inference bothersome to her. The paradox was the blasting from Warren's room; he was consumed with hard rock, a doubling of standards exercised with consistency.

The music of the day held relevance to my identity. It was imperative I be alert of the latest popular tunes, my father helping me. On Saturday afternoons broadcasts of Casey Cassem's America's Top 40 hits came on. While I listened, I wanted the convenience of recording the show so my father set up his reel-to-reel. In the surround sound of headphones my ears glued to private concerts by some of the greatest, their songs to be my generation's classics. I was thankful that my father openly appreciated versatile styles and the qualities of brilliance in modern lyrics.

He got tickets for the whole family to the new show *Hair.* He may have known about the tiny bit of nudity, but he would not make mention of it as my mother would have objected to our seeing the production. The scene was so quick but she was shocked, my father subduing her while promoting the beautification of the au naturel coupled with chuckles. He treated me and Warren to another excellent show, subsequent to its opening in 1969, The Who's rock opera *Tommy.* My mother was not interested in going.

♥   ♥

At thirteen I started the first of four years of study at the Hebrew Academy in Los Angeles, three days a week I on a bus commute shared with peers from the Temple. It surprised me to see one particular boy because his family did not show the appearance of being observant. For the majority of kids, their parents thought this an arrangement good for keeping them away from trouble. Had they only glimpsed lascivious activities aboard the bus, their heads might spin.

I had such a crush on this handsome bad boy who had a conceit of irresistibility. I tried at not being obvious, or so I told myself, but I could not stop looking at him. He, on the other hand, answering my attempted advances by treating me as invisible made me more heated. I was going to make him see the wisdom of his ways. In noticing me, my nervousness was apparent; I was a sucker for his perfunctory flattery, the slightest nod. He was older, into chicks, and although I wished myself fast, I was not about to let myself be used by someone uncaring. It might have been pronounced, my low confidence, but I did have some pride.

The lounge in the building was rarely occupied, but it had a couch, and during breaks we met there, me sitting with his head resting in my lap, a pathetic routine holding little conversation; tiring of that he went in search of some hanky-panky elsewhere.

CHAPTER 12

I was not a troublemaker, but I also could not allow my curiosity being obstructed. Ignorance would not be my bliss. While self-respect and discipline would be my guide for several more years until absolutely certain I was ready, self-education would suffice. Of course any inference of a boyfriend was out of bounds, my mother stopping the idea of my liking someone. I had no realization of how difficult it was going to be for me to have a boy honestly like me.

Wearing my heart on my sleeve, I felt a lot of anger regarding my mother. We were enmeshed in a civil war, I sweating blood to have her embrace me compassionately to allow me safe space for sharing with her. Yet, the older I got the more I realized our relationship was emotionally inhibiting. This circumstance drove me to employing the tactic of self-preservation about what, if anything, I would disclose, or risk losing myself entirely. I could not imagine my mother not loving me, but the signs spoke differently, any sharing to be spit on by her vintage blindness.

Manipulating my development, it took all of my energy trying to stay guarded from her destructive tendencies. She was unbalanced. My mother I could not trust, feeling in my best interest to withdraw, even lie when necessary, deflecting my soul's needs from punishment.

♥   ♥

My father worked extremely hard trying to keep his family happy, enduring his responsibilities seeming to require superhuman strength. Travel being fulfilling, our first was to Seattle's World Fair. He held up his promise that every other summer we would spend in England. We went once to Scandinavia and Holland, to Israel twice, and to iconic and historic spots throughout California. As if turning over a new leaf, my mother finding ease in her skin with a more pleasant disposition.

♥   ♥

Using language succinctly was a process that I had been honing, all along words holding the power to uplift or demean. I heard them seriously, thinking before speaking to not hurt the feelings of others. In spite of ongoing pleas that my mother quit her preponderance of nasty speaking, she returned with, *"I never said anything of the sort."* Not dissuaded, she threw in a second punch, *"You don't know what you're talking about."* My father would not show up to support me, in these treacherous incidents upholding his weary peacemaker position, to everyone's detriment.

♥   ♥

I felt very far removed from a happy-go-lucky child, my inadequacy in fitting in with my peers the precursor to my virtual invisibility, on the fringe. The best way I felt to overcome my self-consciousness was taking the path of least resistance. I would invest my energy in my favorite aspiration, music. *I've got more talent in my pinky than most people have in their entire body.* Okay, I sound conceited but I reasoned it close to actuality.

Entering West Covina High School in September of 1971, at fifteen, I felt like an alien, deficient of titillation for inclusion with the popular— cheerleaders, football stars—no matter how much I may have desired such embracing. No. My ownership was to my authentic nerd and to them I would gravitate. Hand in hand with my required courses, I took music history and theory. Music was in my blood, my centering against the perpetual strain on my existence.

I did not have an issue with my body image, that is, not from the neck down. I found my facial appearance to be, unfortunately, less than satisfactory, and angered with my mother's unreasonable opinions as to what is proper. While she was a vision of perfection, she was oblivious to the way I looked and my feeling ogre-like. I would venture into the smoky den of the girl's bathroom to don lipstick. I hated my natural curly, half-moon do, horribly imitating an afro, using straightening methods that were not lasting.

My hormones were screaming, emboldening me into displays of assertiveness and rebellion. My mother could not relate to my swinging emotions, incapable of recalling her growing pains. Instead of seeing the legitimate cry of mental distress, she presumed I was ill and had me seen by a medical doctor, my condition a hyperthyroid.

How convenient for my mother to have an answer. With the tiniest nodule I was prescribed medication. Still, I doubted this ailment as the sole cause of my disagreeable emotionality. For five years I took the pills in the hope of ensured normality, the effectuality, a protuberance of one of my eyes. While slight, it only helped to accentuate my poor analysis. *Why couldn't I, instead, have had my teeth straightened?*

I developed an even deeper connection to my truer self the next year, leaping forward in proximity to dreams. I would meet my first love in my world history class.

♥   ♥

A most profound aspect of Jewish membership is the responsibility we uphold in our representation. We carry the torch in memorializing the inconceivable atrocities of the six million of our tribe exterminated in The Holocaust; we pay homage to the myriad throughout Jewish history with our people's demise met at the hands of anti-Semites and haters generally—year 5779 and counting.

It is one thing to be taught the generational sorrows and wear the survivors' woes, as we would all loved ones. I was not prepared for the visceral pain that enveloped my body when in sophomore history class a requirement was to watch newsreels of concentration camp prisoners near to death and ovens with murdered children and huge piles of bodies laid one upon another in trenches....

In solemnity and tenderheartedness I feel for any in the throes of suffering, but this history is my heartbreak. It was impossible for me to hide my emotions, my clenched jaw not enough restraint for the tears streaming down my face. I quickly felt the soft touch of a hand on my shoulder and turned around to look into the eyes of the boy sitting directly behind me, his own welling up. After class we had lunch together. With no lull in conversation, akin to having known each other our entire lives, it felt incredible, such a cute guy in my company. His gentle kindness admirable, it seemed easy for him to look past limitations in my looks.

His formal name was Terrence but Terry to friends. He was a charmer, incredibly funny, a great singer, and a phenomenal dancer. His English parents had resettled in Toronto, Canada raising their teenage daughter when he came into the world, after which time they moved, again, to live in West Covina.

He was a most amazing human being, and that he was not Jewish made absolutely no difference. I recall us talking one day about the essence of all religions involving a spiritual search to connect with a higher entity, and thus, we all of the same fabric.

He was also extremely supportive. When divulging my contentious relationship with my mother, he shared he similarly felt an emotional detachment from his father. His parents, like mine, were old school, even as life in Canada was hardly different from that in the States.

I told him that I could sing and before long we were ditching P.E.—we both hated it—and singing to hits filling the radio as we headed to our favorite hangout, Bob's Big Boy Restaurant. He told me he was a member of the high school performing choral group and, since auditions were coming up, I should try out. This was not a classical choir. With dance numbers and skits, they performed at various civic organizations like the Kiwanis and Rotary clubs.

He convinced me that I had the right stuff and I was not passing up this fabulous opportunity. In his interest he was capturing my heart. I was falling in love but I was not about to jeopardize the present, locking away this secret.

I was tremendously excited and believed I could be chosen for this group. I approached my mother once I got home expecting, unwisely, to hear her excitement for me reciprocated. When that did not happen, I retreated to my room to prepare my convincing presentation to my father. Like the racehorse anxious for release from the start gate, before I had a chance my mother readied her aggressive pounce.

He understood my passionate longing to be part of this group, yet confrontation with my mother had to ensue. Her unease: since Friday night performances were required, what possible explanation would suffice about my nonattendance on the *shul* choir? What about singing carols at Christmastime? My father rebutted my mother's reaching with the rationale one is not made a believer simply by the act. *Right on, Dad*, I thought, from the depths happiness welling up.

I wanted this; tasting its vital importance. I decided on auditioning before an onslaught of unwarranted scrutiny by my mother, based on a ridiculous fear of the congregation aghast!

With only a week before tryouts, my mother rabidly argued against me, while my father was unbelieving at her cold-heartedness and refusal to loosen her constraint over me.

Decisive about this win I attended the audition having not received the backing from my mother to evidence her being in my corner. I chose the song "I'll Never Fall in Love Again" by Dionne Warwick, and nailed it. My reward was seeing Terry's gleeful expression.

I had won; what could my mother do about it now?

♥   ♥

When Warren was fifteen he and his best friend of the same age were preparing for a road trip to San Diego for over a week in the summer. They were not driving as they had yet no permits, but riding unsophisticated bikes there and back. My mother waived all concerns so as not to deny him his wish. Neither could foresee the extent of this blessing.

CHAPTER 13

My father was in the kitchen helping my mother put the finishing touches on dinner when I approached. Unable to hold back my emotions, *"I made it in! I was good enough."* My father's smile reflected mine, but my mother was only capable of throwing up her hands with a big huff. Hostile in her surrender, her damnation causing my father's face to change in resignation. I was not about going along with my mother's intentions for my life. I felt my parents' scorn at not listening to their wishes.

I should have been capable of getting past the hurt, my mother's refused support eating at my confidence, she vigorous with her humiliation.

At sixteen, I was graduating from the Academy and hoping to join my fellow classmates on a summer *ulpan* to Israel, three months living and working on a kibbutz while also touring throughout the country. Partly funded, the trip was offered in acknowledgment for the accomplishments of its graduates. My hopes were dashed with my mother's retort, *"You're too young."* The age of my classmates, she again holding me back from a celebration I had earned.

My mother's obvious assault on my image showing what little faith she held when it came to me.

My father eagerly accepted the task of teaching me to drive. I did not think it a problem learning the use of the clutch, my smarts and go-getter attitude all I would need.

♥   ♥

I was a member of the Chamber Singers during my junior and senior years allowing my relationship with Terry to get closer. When hanging out we had great fun, but no advances came, even as my attraction was apparent. He was a huge fan of swing dancing and I was bent on being his main partner; he would touch me then. I quickly got in step, he immensely pleased. Closing out my seventeenth year I could more easily excuse my going out to dance the night away with Terry, he meaning the world to me and I feeling true vitality.

I knew he had a girlfriend for as long as we had known each other but having not witnessed them together got me believing I harnessed the power to make him want me.

He showed up with her at a Chamber Singers party and I, stupidly, anticipated he would spend some time with me. He acted like a typical male. I might as well have not been there. While romantic music filled the summer atmosphere, I was becoming extremely upset; my fault to expect from him that for which I was pining but yet shown.

My inexperience in the realm of relationships made me gullible, unprotected against my heart being broken. It was all in or nothing, in a vulnerable place I showering on myself no mercy.

Across the street from our house was a park. Often after dark I would leave the house, making the excuse I was meeting a girlfriend to study, Terry similarly fabricating his retreat from his parents' demands. Out of place near the playground was fixed a giant steel culvert pipe. Secluding ourselves inside it seemed to make the best rendezvous.

I had exhausted my patience, needing to know why he would not put his arm around me or affectionately kiss me. I had imagined the moment, looking glamorous in his company. We sat close one night talking and laughing, losing track of time. I leaned in to kiss him, he backed away. He did not like me that way.

The gamble did not pay off in the form of attention I was seeking. Terry wanted to preserve all we had; I knew our friendship was most important. We pretended nothing had changed. Our bond impenetrable, we valued our relationship dearly and would be there for each other.

It would take three years for the answer of why any romantic love I longed for him to reciprocate would never occur.

♥   ♥

I am grateful being Jewish. I grew up appreciating the deeper teachings of the Torah and Talmud with their influencing every aspect of our humanity. The Jewish people's experience has been the ceaseless wielding of horrific pain and loss, across generations a manufacturing of propaganda spewing unjustifiable harm. Yet in faith we persevere and strive for decency, with perpetual vigilance saving us from ultimate extinction.

When Warren and I were youngsters, one neighbor boy called us the fascist term *"dirty Jews"* while we played innocently in our front yard. His mental violence, meant to frighten, did not result in a life-threatening act, thank God. Still, it evidenced a proliferation of learned behavior long after the demise of Hitler.

♥   ♥

In the midst of his returning from his wonderful trip, Warren was bracing for a conversation he could no longer dodge. He had been dealing with a nagging ache deep in his left shoulder that apparently came on after a fall while he played basketball months before. He anxiously wanted a doctor's opinion. A battery of tests followed plus analyses by several physicians, our parents' worst fears realized.

Warren had contracted the extremely rare primary bone malignancy with the official name of Osteosarcoma, this cancer often choosing children and young adults with exposure to some form of radiation in the womb.[6]

How could we come to grips with this unspeakable diagnosis?

The severe nature of Warren's condition left only a short span of time for all of us to internalize this crisis and the expert directive. The doctors believed the best assurance for complete removal of this tumor required Warren's entire left arm amputation. Earth's floor had split open beneath us, we were in hell, the faith of our parents crumbling.

My mother was in denial, not willing to connect the dots. The truth was staring her in the face; it was a result of her having chosen radioactive iodine as the remedy in fighting her thyroid problem.

As devastating as it was the circumstance affecting his mortality, his strength galvanized his decisiveness. He wanted all of the relevant facts

---

6   Excerpted from the CDC clinician fact sheet: "...the human embryo and fetus are particularly sensitive to ionizing radiation.... Such consequences can include...cancer."

of which the doctors never hesitated to give him, including the risks of going forward and what would follow: an intensive program of radiation and chemotherapy. He was such an inspiration, refusing any pity. He adamantly stomped on any doubts, certain of his ability to do everything just as he had before.

It was decided Warren would receive post-surgical cancer therapy at the City of Hope, it renowned with the success of curing many with the disease. Interesting to note is the common treatment of radiation— although possibly more powerful in killing the cancer cells, it would be stopped, while chemotherapy, known to cause the most debilitation, continued.

He accomplished exactly what he had envisioned, playing basketball, riding a bike and just plain living to his absolute fullest, using his prosthetic arm infrequently. The competence of all the doctors overshadowed the reality that even after all Warren had sustained there was no surety of the cancer being completely obliterated.

One year passed, then two, with him in and out of the hospital, courageously tolerating the unbearable pain, while we endlessly prayed and hoped with every ounce of our beings that he would beat a death sentence.

Functioning in the midst of overwhelming distress my father's focus remained on his responsibilities of work and keeping stability at home. He and my mother were, incredibly, unable to conceive of my own fears at seeing Warren's suffering.

"Don't do as I do, do as I say." With the intensity of Warren's ordeal I was expected to shut down my feelings, as usual they irrelevant.

We could not realize how destructive the effects of chemotherapy would be on such a physically strong person as Warren. Now his cancer had metastasized, diminishing all certainty of his survival.

When not in the hospital he was home, bedridden. My bedroom was adjacent to his and much of the time he could not sleep. His pain causing tremendous discomfort, he had fits of coughing as fluid was entering his lungs. He was dying in front of our eyes, yet we were oppressed in our ability to accept the tragedy unfolding of this beautiful boy slipping away. His life could not end before his wings had barely opened.

CHAPTER 14

Graduating high school I started courses at Mount San Antonio Community College. In an English class there sat behind me a girl named Leslie. I knew her from the *shul* and I figured, like many in the congregation, she knew my family's misery. I felt unable to talk about it, my preferring to avoid any pity. Yet, my attempts at acting antisocial did not register with her. As much as she cared to know how I was fairing, she also relentlessly asked for my advice about grammar and spelling. She was smart, seeing this tack might bring us closer, and it did. One day our conversation turned to the idea of our taking a trip to Israel. My preformed opinion of her had been in error, as I soon came to realize. As our friendship quickly grew, it became clear how lucky I was in having let her into my life.

We were bound that coming summer of 1976 on an *ulpan* to Israel, at twenty, this adventure finally allowable. Meanwhile, my father had arranged to take Warren to see the Summer Olympic Games in Montreal. He had bought the tickets a year earlier hoping for the trip to be a catalyst in warding off Warren's decline, and it worked for the time they were there.

Leslie and I also had the time of our lives, but when we got back it was to learn Warren's circumstances were dire. One night I called her asking if she wanted to go to a club with me, not to dance; I needed escape. I proceeded to get violently drunk and during the drive home extremely nauseous.

Rushing through the doorway, it was impossible to hide my condition from my mother and I vomited all over the floor. Exploding accusatorily, *"You're going out to have a good time while your brother is dying in the next room!"*

My mother would not forgive me, maintaining my behavior proved I did not care. I remain mystified at her refusal not to understand how terribly alone, how sad, I was, my father not amending her misconception. In her estimation it was one more example of my selfishness, my feelings invalid. My friends I could count on in sharing my sorrow, but not my mother.

♥　　　♥

My first dutiful employment was at the *Los Angeles Times* telephone marketing office during my two years in junior college, successfully grossing high numbers of subscriptions. Of course, I was still intending on imprinting my name on the musical stage, but that was down the road. In the meantime, I needed to increase my income with my plan establishing a more lucrative line of work as a secretary, my typing top notch.

My mother was no more proud of this decision than others I had made—she had her ideas of what I should do for a living, which ultimately would require more education which would thwart my making money, which would mean I would have to live at home.

♥　　　♥

My mother and father refused to give up on another possible treatment which might still save Warren. Laetrile, an organic remedy, was effective in combating cancers in other countries, but in the United States the Federal Drug Administration had not approved of its use here. Tijuana, Mexico was the closest city having an innovative and legal treatment program. By now, Warren's deterioration was to the point he was given less than a couple of weeks to live, his body ravaged, the worst nearing.

Bearing the heat of summer it was my parents' last push to get him to the hospital there.

Leslie went with me to see him one time and it was very difficult for me. Having been so over-protected, living in a world of idealism, his dying was not something I could truly wrap my brain around. My heart was breaking to see him in such bad shape, so frail his frame barely visible in his wheelchair. I wanted only to believe when I next saw him he would be home and well.

Miraculously, Warren exceeded all prediction, living another month, holding on until a few days after he would have graduated high school. On June 16, 1977, following three brutalizing years, he surrendered into God's arms, resting in final peace, at just eighteen.

♥   ♥

Being perfect in a little while he fulfilled long years
Warren's headstone inscription

Ancient religions hold the belief of trees inhabited by gods. My father had long found enrapture at the intricacy of their branches entwine, their magnificence spreading up to the skies. The burial place of Warren is up the grassy knoll of Burbank's Mount Sinai Memorial Park Cemetery, its view the Hollywood Hills, its protection a gorgeous cedar.

Regardless of the time one might be given, no one is prepared for the inconceivable outcome. I would never see my brother in life again, the fateful call from my father. In his unrepressed shaky voice telling me Warren was gone, but before dying requesting my father convey his words, *"tell Alene I love her,"* knowing his love granting me solace, a memorializing of the truth if not always having been recognizable.

Like humpty dumpty, my fairytale shelling broken, it was unbearable to handle this alone. I needed Terry, who answered my call. I felt his sympathy, I could trust him to come and get me away, where immaterial. Frankly, I only remember my immense gratefulness at his rescuing me in my grief.

Warren has come into my dreams, once seeing his face in a beautiful smile messaging he was okay; I still sense his aura, one of my angels.

CHAPTER 15

The millions of tears my mother would cry over her son's death could never sufficiently fill the well of her guilt.

"There is no greater pain than losing a child."

I had no way of totally comprehending my parents' desolation. Where once fulfillment and hopes abounded in the vitality of their fun-loving, fiercely energetic son, the magnitude of his absence from our world would leave the everlasting crater of anguish.

When Warren died, I quickly decided that it was my responsibility to be the strong one for my parents. I did as much as possible to help them talk about their feelings. It was up to me I felt to somehow make up for their loss, like that was within my capacity. Their sorrow was immediate. I had enough worldly intelligence to effectuate my ability to process this tragedy I convinced myself; I should act grownup. I was now twenty-one.

The death of a child either brings a couple closer or tears their union asunder. My mother expressed her grief without losing faith—she could not fool herself by cursing God. The existence of a higher power for my father in this tragedy was a conflict unresolved. On uncountable days, he leant comfort in service to the Temple members. Now, he felt his duty was to put on a strong front in the carriage of his community, bearing his despondency in private.

I heard the words from my mother's lips, incapable of self-restraint from this awful indignation: *"Why couldn't it have been you?"* She tried assuring me that she did not mean it, but I know some part of her did.

Quoted within these pages are many of her scathing remarks. I would not be able to banish from my mind their gravity.

They decided that group therapy with other parents who had lost a child might benefit their healing. Although encouraged at first, they stopped after a few sessions, my mother believing the pain of another in similar despair did not match her agony. I believe she feared full disclosure with strangers who would deduce her culpability. She had to hold close her guilt, believing it proof of the depth of her devotion. Deception ruled her days.

♥   ♥

My father followed my mother, believing I would get over Warren's death and make their future worthwhile. So my life would still be lived from the place of their reliance. They were doing the best they could, but I questioned the myriad contradictions: the love my mother claimed to have for me and her adversarial words and actions.

While carrying out his duties my father took solace from his fellow workers and people at the *shul*. In his decision to stay married he held the inevitability that any happiness would be scorched, resigned in fatalism. His purpose had always been giving help to others, beginning and ending with consoling my mother who could not look beyond her pain neither for him nor her present living daughter.

I mistakenly took the duty of being responsible and placing my parents' grief above my own. They neglected to offer professional assistance to me, thus mirroring their clueless rationale for hiding me from the experience of my reality. *"The less you know the better."* Screaming inside, I begged the growth of my emotional intellect.

In Judaism this sentiment is paid to one mourning: *May his memory be a blessing.* It is not meant to curse, yet my mother's will was only staying lost in her sorrow for too many years, adding to my father's emotional distress, before feeling it alright to break out into hearty laughter or allow dancing. She believed she must sacrifice happiness for the sake of her son, her first, last and every thought in between. She feared otherwise she would forget him as if that could ever be possible.

This would not have been Warren's want, they lost in a martyrdom and not locking his imprint in time, with a charity perhaps in his name, making a purposeful difference in bettering another's future, as many people determine as rewarding in the maintenance of one's memory.

My father would spend ten years on the manuscript of his life story, albeit erring on misinterpreting incidents involving me and, with the wager of my mother's scrutiny, ensuring my bad representation, a vehement denial of my person from their convenient selective memory. The book would never go further than its drafting.

♥   ♥

Ten years earlier Daddy Low had died from a heart condition, and sharing my room was Nana, she visiting for frequent stretches. Her buoyant heart had been changed yet she had carried on with a benevolence ruling. Just months after Warren's passing, a stroke took her.

Might the earthly to celestial conduit be but a wire?

♥   ♥

Terry knew he had to take the risk to be completely open and honest to prevent our friendship from dissolving. Having moved to Hollywood after graduating high school with an ambition to work in the entertainment industry, he wanted a career as a wardrobe consultant. With his first gig dressing comedian Jonathan Winters he secured one of several long-term clients.

We scheduled a date to meet at his new place. We relaxed, had drinks, and famished we walked down the block to the Astral Burger, planting ourselves on the patio. He then opened up about his attraction to boys from early age, his feelings eclipsed from fright. With homophobia at a height in the late '70s, "coming out" was a daunting task.

"I love you, everything's okay."

The color rushed back to his face, a relief in his smile. He had been tormented, horrified at what his parents would think as their Episcopalian faith would make acceptance unlikely. Feeling the chains unwrapping, his body loosening up, he was trusting on my knowing the truth not cracking our foundation. It never would.

It effectuated little shock, I suspecting it the reason for choosing out of any intimacy. Admittedly, I was happy for confirmation of my not being a turnoff. He had spent years in that illusion of a straight image; his comportment showing no effeminacy; when he included me in his circle of male friends, my ego was misdirected, he only wanting to assure my special place amongst his friendships.

As for memorable adventures, one was notably fantastic. It was October 1974 and Terry and I were off to the Forum in Inglewood for a concert headlining Elton John, who was touring with Kiki Dee—remember "Don't Go Breaking My Heart"?—rapturous over the *Yellow Brick Road* album, his performances legendary. Terry, such a big part of my life, had served in validating my capacity for having and being a true unconditional friend. Now, many years subsequent to high school, our vitality together was intensified.

We kept dancing. A frequent brunch spot was The French Market, with its delightful New Orleans ambiance and exceptional food. Also, we toured the *Queen Mary* in Long Beach, the vessel on which I had reached America. In 1978, while Terry was on an extended stay in England, Leslie and I took the opportunity of a summer holiday there, and as we hoped it was a wild time.

As expected, my mother's heart palpitations did not lesson much when it came to my relationship with Terry. Even after learning there would be no involvement. I was not his type, she could rest assured. But irrational unease consumed her thoughts: he was a non-Jew. I was not falling for her repeated ignorance.

♥　　　♥

I was desperate to leave my parents' home. Long adult in the eyes of the law, at twenty-two my mother anticipated my staying until I married. Trying to preserve my sanity was of the absolute necessity. I would have to get a job that hopefully paid well, which meant passing on my graduating junior college with only a few quarters to go. The urgency for freedom and a supposed granting of my rightful chance at living my own life was acute.

"Once you leave this house you'll never be allowed back!" This was my mother's shining exclamation when I walked out. On some level she was again experiencing loss, but in fact, our rift had only grown, she incapable of any encouragement towards my well-being, even as I was just beginning on my life's journey.

I had begun my executive assistant career. Commuting into the city an hour each way was exhausting. In Van Nuys I found a cheap apartment, mainly in preparation of my parents wanting to visit. I was not staying there much since dating an Israeli guy, Avi, for a while. It was all I imagined an ideal relationship to be.

A bit older and extremely good looking, he was actually falling for me. He had attained citizenship upon deciding to make his home in "The Valley" permanent, since being here achieving his command of English. He was estranged from his parents living in Iraq but extremely close with his two sisters and a nephew living nearby. I began to ponder could he be the one; I must be sure. We decided to move in together under the condition my parents not getting wind of it.

With much in common his happiness convinced me of my own. I was enamored by the kind of love of which a woman only dreams, his affection, his words, comforting. He was ambitious seeking a burgeoning entrepreneurship as a landscape designer and house painter. I got on well with his family, but what I had not realized was the error of exchanging housemates instead of going it alone and proactively seeking emotional fitness. Rose-colored glasses made perfect the picture.

As if a brilliant constellation puncturing her sphere of lamentation, once more my mother looked to me for her wish fulfillment. Nearing two years together, the nature of my relationship with Avi had become clear. My father was instructed to inquire of his intentions.

Amidst the glowing romance, the more I had gotten to know him, I found myself fighting doubts about his true feelings for me. He could be condescending, bringing me to tears with his dismissal, simulating the behavior of my mother, his narcissism barely conquerable; he apologetic, we would be back in each other's arms.

He felt up against the wall at my father's requesting some disclosure. He spoke convincingly, stating he and I had discussed a formal engagement that appeared likely, to be announced in the not-too-distant future. As soon as my mother was told this she called me aside to talk. She wanted to hear from me how I felt about Avi becoming my husband. Having been too sheltered with no real sense of what an intimate relationship should look like I was over the moon that he had deep feelings.

"You probably should marry him; you're not likely to be asked again," my mother said. Not a rousing applause in fortification of her favor on me. With planning begun, in her belief an Israeli was the most observant. In fact, the opposite is true for the majority of its populace, a spiritual connect exempting requisite observance. I would not let her know this. I felt the ropes release. I could now own my personal faith without the fear of reproach.

Avi wanted to do right by my father but his manner of popping the question did not follow that shown to most women. Not yearning while on one knee, just *"How about if we get married?"* Oh well, I thought, not worth making a fuss over.

♥   ♥

It was my wedding but my mother was completely in charge, the message subliminal. I had virtually no say. The Cantor's daughter would be having the congregation in attendance. I was in on the design of invitations and aside from shopping for a dress that the extent of consultation.

My mother poured herself into this dream occasion, with my father's wholehearted agreement in throwing a lot of money into making it the whirlwind affair she wanted. I, naively, still believing they were doing this for my benefit, with my interests the sole basis of each decision.

When meeting with Avi's sisters a few times, to the dismay of my mother they were smart, seeing through her shallow exterior. This was about her as usual, not me, not Avi. Her recourse was dismissive, they were impolite and argumentative. Any interests of importance to them were inconsequential, such a showy ceremony to impress not at the top of Avi's preference.

It was obvious my being powerless in opposing my parents. Avi and I felt a better send off was satisfying the need of a reliable car. He tried broaching the subject with my father who minimized its immediacy, but Avi would not back off, pressing *"We must have this before we can go ahead with the wedding."* The necessity real, nonetheless I tried to convince him that my father was listening and on top of it; his sisters defending his adamancy, his mind was unchanged.

The night before the wedding, Avi called to restate the ultimatum. I stressed my father was near to finalizing a purchase, while unbearable his threatening not to marry me before the matter concluded. *How could he do this to me?* His insensitivity shockingly wrong on every level, my tears unstoppable, on the phone in my parents' bedroom they heard the conversation. They tried to calm me, but in no way was I marrying a man who puts the value of a car over me! In my gut I resolute to that the best decision, my mother then summing up her real feelings: *"The invitations are all out, we can't cancel the wedding now!"*

♥   ♥

It was my day, one to marvel in memory, I believed. I honestly knew Avi was a decent man if not without flaws like me. I had to believe after marriage our bond would be enhanced with more compassion. I could change him. My ideas of what I was getting into absent its reality.

Sunday, October 21, 1979 was filled with glamour. All were decked out in the finest of wear, ripe for portraits as the hues of autumn's leaves were falling like confetti in the bright sunlight. Of course, I had followed through with the obligatory rituals prior to the day, like a virginal bathing at the *mikva*, and I was aware of the ceremonial aspect of my circling my soon-to-be husband seven times in respect for him and his wishes. Suddenly, there was a pause, my father interjecting a prayer in memory of Warren. I had no inkling. Remembering him was certainly important and expected at the reception. It was I under that *chuppah*, this moment mine. My parents had chosen to give me no exclusivity.

♥   ♥

While Avi and I honeymooned in Las Vegas the car was bought. I think my father resented having to dish out additional money after the wedding expense, but he knew it necessary, my mother's distaste about Avi's family only exacerbated.

Back in the groove of our daily life it was not long before the bliss dissipated and disgruntlement set in. Avi seemingly looked for reasons to negate my intelligence, he unchanged despite my hope. Misunderstandings were becoming a regular upheaval with blame squarely on me, in my familiarity with such treatment I resigned in apology. It was impossible to accept what was happening.

What was the cause of our fleeting happiness, his elusive compassion? At times we related positively but I could not shake my internal heartbreak. I had to fix this. I suggested we get therapy but only once he went with me before deciding he did not need it, his inference, it was my problem. For my well-being I continued, although coming to terms with the truth hard.

I had in actuality married a domineering person, a wakeup call not to be ignored. Although we were fine as friends, our union had not worked to mutual benefit. It should never have happened as it was doomed from the start. At the end of two years we separated; with time apart the importance of being married would be revived. Yet, further delving into my wanting, the more powerful were the revelations about my damaging past.

♥   ♥

Like clockwork my menstruation came regularly, so when I missed one soon after the split I was suspicious. I bought a test, the result positive. In shock initially, I knew I must don my rational cap.

Terrified at the prospect of rebuke from my mother, her perilous domineering in violation of all boundaries, it was with a heavy heart that I made a decision. In spite of our marriage seemingly irreconcilable, Avi wanted me to carry to full term. I felt it would be unfair to have the child be without two parents. I believed, at only six weeks, God would forgive me for my choosing to abort. In my time of need Avi was understanding and supported me, in some respect he, too, relieved.

I honestly felt it was the best solution. In hindsight, it may be my one regret as I am sympathetic with children, they sensing my affection. It would have killed my parents to ever tell this secret, but staying faithful to this story is of great imperative. I simply could not muster the courage in taking the high road and owning the ramifications.

♥   ♥

I soon found out Avi had reconnected with his old flame, while keeping up with manipulative suggestions of wanting to save the marriage. I was terribly confused, my thinking swaying back and forth out of my control. I could not trust in confidence. After two and a half years of limbo my decision certain, accepting failure notwithstanding, my courage found. By staying together my life was continuing its descent into irrevocable torment. I had to save myself, even if that meant living alone for the rest of my life.

I had been afraid of telling my parents we might not make it. Surely, my mother would be extremely upset and worried about the opinions of others. I would be made to feel obligated whatever the emotional impact, imagining their emphasized disappointment doubting the credibility of my feelings. Rather surprising was receiving from them their assurance in support of my decision.

My marriage was declared over on the fifteenth day of August 1984. I was twenty-eight yet emotionally having weathered a lifetime of storms. My mother could not have known the effect of her self-fulfilling prophecy that I would not be fortunate to marry again.

From left, my maternal grandparents, Maurice and Dolly Low, and Mr. and Mrs. Lapp, Enid's parents, at the engagement party of Herbert and his bride-to-be.

Me at two years old with my few playthings.

A professional photograph of me at age 6 and Warren at age 3.

It is the summer of 1969 and Warren, at age 10, is king of the world in Swansea Park, across from our grandparents' home.

Nana and me on a family summer holiday near Lake Tahoe in 1970. The Ponderosa Ranch was a theme park based on the TV show *Bonanza*.

Herbert in a happy embrace with Enid and their children, from left Andrea, Marc, and Julian, in the backyard of their home in Cardiff, South Wales. I believe this trip to Great Britain was in January 1974.

Me at age 18 and Warren at age 15 in Haifa, Israel. This was a happy and carefree family trip in January 1974, a pivotal year with Warren's cancer diagnosis that summer.

From left, Terry, me, Leslie, and Terry's boyfriend headed for a night of dancing at a London disco in 1978.

Performing a duet with my father at one of the *shul* fundraisers.

This is the handsome beige tabby I adopted soon after moving to Seattle. In black and white the picture does not do his beauty justice.

From left, my father, mother, Herbert, and Enid.

My mother and me in 2012 with Enid outside the flat just blocks from the ocean in Bournemouth, England, this trip my final visit with my dear Uncle Herbert.

Leslie and me outside of her home a few years back.

CHAPTER 16

With a portfolio of headshots I took every chance to make real my professional goal. I attended a commercial workshop. I acted in community musical theatre and sang in groups. My father helped me put together a cassette of twelve tracks accompanied by his pianist plus a machine with other orchestral instruments. He had made an album so I hoped to promote the tape for the same reason. Only I needed to seek the financial backing of an agent to have it go anywhere.

I knew I was good, but that good?

My father gladly shared his marvelous voice giving concerts at Jewish homes for the aged. For six years, he sponsored annual fundraising shows at *shul.* My mother was the influencer of the repertoire of love ballads. Besides duets with each of us, I enjoyed center stage showcasing my own stylistic collection. My mother had no issue about my singing as long as it was not professionally.

There were few occasions when my parents came to see me in a show or concert that did little to erase their disapproval at my striving towards a musical career. My mother's claim of worry about the rejection often parceled out was an attempt to dissuade me; in another breath this: *"Why is it so hard for you to complete anything?"*

The noise in my head was her vitriol, its intrusion a persistent block to my capacity to trust in my own mind, to have faith in my own ability, to not fear success! I never wanted to believe I was deceiving myself but unshakable were my lingering doubts, my efforts finally suppressed.

♥   ♥

New professional and personal challenges were in store to transform my experience of life in ways I could not have anticipated.

I had become employed at a well-known collection agency in West Los Angeles, diligently arranging financial settlements. I did not want my sadness being obvious but the end of my marriage the worst feeling, one more death. Sitting across the aisle was Su who could not help but see I was in a bad place. As I opened up she was empathetic. The demise of her two marriages had become the catalyst for seeking further growth. We got on well, I trusted in her caring, and she had an answer to my woes.

She was involved in a program called Lifespring. It was not a tearing down of one's emotions, like EST, or the cult mentality of Scientology, but a loving and experiential training of enlightenment and self-discovery.

It sounded great but I was dubious. Besides, it was expensive, just the beginner's course. Living paycheck to paycheck I would have to ask my father for help to enroll. I was proceeding to find my own place to live. She had a two-bedroom apartment in Torrance near the beach. She asked of my interest in moving in with her and I jumped at the idea, but it would take further convincing of the value of joining the program. In the end I did.

Our friendship led me to getting close to her inner circle, people like myself having experienced a darker life. I had found a family. I was in the program for five years. I learned a great deal, a rebirthing to help reinforce strength of mind and body, and the goodness of humanity. I went on wilderness adventures, rappelled down a mountain. I stretched to climb a tall tree to grasp a high hanging ring. I fell backwards in faith to be caught.

More than any other period in my life I participated in service projects including variety shows benefitting the March of Dimes, escorting people with cerebral palsy on day outings at Disneyland and helping to prepare celebrations at a home for abused and neglected children. I became especially attached to one woman with CP who had no family. Although the facility where she lived was quite a distance drive I often visited. Using my language art skills, I got ESL certified and was a tutor.

Ultimately, I got infuriated; facing everything I went through again conjuring up such rage, like a foreign entity rising up and out from my soul. The experience had been healing, but for the unfinished business remaining with me and my mother. Expressing my thoughts in writing and in person, I needed her full comprehension of her emotional damage on my life and her apology. I was expecting our relationship, from this point, to be one based on honesty.

"You're mentally ill." My mother's reaction was not budging from her position, refusing any admittance of fault or vulnerability. Her incapacity to verbalize she was sorry for any detrimental impact on my development as a character flaw of hers, she was rendering my mental state as the singular cause of my life's pain. Making this about a shortcoming of mine felt impossible to forgive.

"Have I really been such a terrible mother?"

You, the reader, decide. She was still not listening, but I could not bring myself to flatly condemn her.

My father's stance was backing her, firmly resorting to disfavor at my communiqués, *"What a diatribe!"*

I had had enough. I had no connection to them. In title only, they were my parents, but not in any actions that visibly benefitted my self-worth. We were estranged for a year, one of several instances when it was imperative that I completely separate from them. I was still holding hope that they would wake up and celebrate me and my efforts, rather than seeing me as an utter disappointment. Surely, one day I would receive acceptance from my mother. Yet, I was being taken down a peg with no rights to complain. After all the money my father had footed for my wedding, my car, my keep....

No amount of appreciation on my part could satisfy as in their estimation my gratitude debt was huge, plus my mother's repeated gripe at not giving her grandchildren was further shaming my failings relative to her wanting.

♥   ♥

Terry's presence in my life was still vitally important and I was committed to doing the utmost in guaranteeing our staying as close. I moved to Hollywood's Fairfax area in 1986. By then he was in love with a fellow whose home was in Britain and decided to emigrate.

Terry returned to California after a couple of years. He had broken off the relationship. It was unfortunate but I was happy to have my dear friend back. Shocking news came weeks later when I learned he was sickened by the Auto Immune Deficiency Syndrome—AIDS!

It was not contagious, the truth, he getting all of my support yet alone praying out of fear he might not survive. In 1988 there did not exist the medicinal regimen we have today to level the playing field and offer a fighting chance of life with this disease. He sought every option available, for over a year his symptomatology appearing to stabilize.

♥   ♥

Listening to my conscience I knew I should reunite with my parents even if I would not feel their claimed love truly. They had lived thirty years in the United States, with every hardship manifesting my mother's restlessness.

Subtlety not her forte, during these years she made no bones that it was this country causing her irascibility, it corrupting the happiness she deserved. My father, finally worn down, would have given her the moon if she asked. The loving husband he had forever been, he was going to find the way to enable their emigration back to England.

Walking around the neighborhood was not unusual, except on this particular July afternoon accompanied by my mother, she eager to get me aside, a burning pressure on her lips. She spilled her anxiety formed as a question, her need assurance about a decision already made.

My father acquired the position of a transcontinental engineering consultant between his company's locations in Israel and the U.S., his employer first paying for several trips to England to allow him to find the house of my mother's dreams—in London's northern outskirts a two-story spread, its spacious backyard looking out on an adjacent golf course—then covering the cost to pack and ship their belongings.

It had been ten years since Warren's death. Only I was left to approve of my parents' arrangement. I met her disclosure unhesitating, sincere in my pleasure at her long sought after desire. Honestly, it was a blessing in disguise.

My mother did inquire as to my considering moving to England, which was odd, as if not cognizant of our real problems, I without the conviction that my upheaval could translate to a satisfactory mend of our relationship. My life's epicenter was America, in childhood, youth, adulthood, a coalescence of British inherited attributes a byproduct.

I didn't have the wherewithal for this do over.

♥ ♥

Terry's treatment proved insufficient in warding off his illness. I saw him one last time; his bathrobe could not conceal the decay to his body. It seemed difficult for him to stand but he did, allowing me a hug, a kiss, an *adieu mi amour*. He was a jewel of a man who had his life robbed too soon!

Almost three months subsequent to his thirty-fourth birthday, on October 29, 1990, Terry passed away.

Cloistered in solitude in my humble apartment, the darkness of night outside my windows drew in boisterous crowds on the sidewalks, the street's volume amplified by the roar of motorcycles and cars. I envied those reveling without any care. *Am I destined for living on the sidelines like a spectator?* I felt myself not quite fitting with society, seeming too different. Feeling totally depressed, I felt my fighting instinct weakening, my compounded fears of inadequacy churning up thoughts of death.

♥ ♥

Aside from Leslie, there was no one keeping me in California anymore. I trusted our friendship would remain strong. Not a fan of the asphalt jungle I, at thirty-five, took a leap of faith. I had long envisioned a more eco-friendly environment to spend, perhaps, the rest of my life, a place with the panorama of beautified scenes in every direction, the answer initiated on a silver platter, seemingly.

Su was now living in Seattle, Washington with her husband and their first child. I missed her and she had given me an open invitation to visit. So I did. As the plane landed I felt an immediate satiation for that imagined. I wished to make this city my new home and knowing someone here was a strong incentive. I started putting in overtime most weekends at a worker's compensation law firm in serious preparation—subsequent to a general secretarial post I had veered to join a placement agency; at six months on a commission basis I had barely accrued any income; it was suggested I apply for this legal job and I nabbed it, a new specialty to propel my pride. Halfway into that year Su's husband, Joe, who was animation supervisor of Pixar, was needed back full time at the California studio.

I was in a quandary, at first unsure if I should leave the comforts I had in place to transition to some unknown. I had to take any fears while going forward with the move. I would let nothing alter my taking the biggest stretch yet. In October of 1991, I drove alone up the coast, across two treacherous mountain passes which sorely challenged my father's old car, my limited belongings in a small attached trailer, over four days my angels willing safe arrival. Su's cousin kindly opened her home to me for three months—although I had submitted resumes before I left California I received no interest, so mightily I proceeded once here to secure a legal assistant position and an apartment.

My mother could easily write complimentary words in birthday cards, a rarity in a letter praising my decision with wishes for my success, wonders never ceasing!

♥   ♥

In twenty-six years in Seattle my fortune's evidence is not a saturation of accoutrements but being in the midst of fine friendships.

I had fresh ambitions to accomplish once here. Preceding this move I had returned to college, wanting to complete my AA in Liberal Arts, which included a feat of passing basic algebra. The rest of my schedule included child development classes, my next invention for a career but one I did not reach; due to financial struggles interfering, it was mandatory I switch priorities to work.

I performed with the Seattle Choral Company for a season. Besides occasional karaoke, I put singing on the back burner to apply my talent to my new avocation as a writer and editor.

Before her first child Su had two cats, brothers. As kittens, I felt an immediate affinity to the one I thought the most adorable if not the more rambunctious. If a scenario arose that required she part with him I promised my adoption. As it turned out she did need me to take Cleager, keeping the docile brother for the safety of her child. At five years old I got him from the plane. He was really amorous, seeking constant attention that I had abundant for thirteen years. I melted at his intelligence, his meows sounding like talking as if he had been a human in another life. Or perhaps, I a cat!

After fifteen years Su and I had a falling out, which does not diminish my gratefulness for such a meaningful time nor how the Lifers inspired in me a stronger sense of my own greatness.

While covering for an absence at a firm, one of the lawyers mentioned about his friend wanting to produce an extensive historical genealogy dating to the 18th century. One co-worker, having seen proof of my meticulous work, piped up to suggest me for the project. I was flattered by the offer, especially after finding out that I was being hired by Microsoft's international sales and marketing director, Jeffrey Raikes.[7]

Subsequent to that success, his brother requested my help on one of his books. That followed with a couple of years as a publisher's assistant. For many years since I have been freelancing, developing other nonfiction works from start to finish.

It has been a dream come true finding my passion in a talent latent much too long.

---

7 Jeff parted from Microsoft to become CEO of the Bill and Melinda Gates Foundation. He and his wife then established the Raikes Foundation, whose emphasis is on the necessity for enhancing the quality of education in every school level, with specific focus the minority and low income populace in the State of Washington.

CHAPTER 17

My father had two choice anthems. The song "My Way," which Paul Anka wrote for Frank Sinatra, alludes to the self-secure man owning his success in spite of his lot. His other signature number, "The Impossible Dream" from the musical *Man of La Mancha* evokes a man's existential quest for extrication from self-imposed emotional shackles to blaze glorious trails in search of great distinction, while dousing the notion of regret.

Don Quixote's chivalrous quality was infatuating to my father. In humility he mastered a courageous destiny, his rapture sowed in the ideals of goodwill and purpose.

I last visited my parents' home in February of 2012. A few months earlier during a physical examination it was discovered that my father had an enlarged prostrate. The medical establishment touts the best remedy against the definite risk of cancer forming in that region is extraction. My father had been free of any serious illness so he would take this action if it averted a further threat to his life.

He had done his homework. He strongly perceived the operation as necessary and went about scheduling it. My mother was against him going through with it, opining on fears of it being a mistake. He had not expected to be waiting four months but doctors were going on strike and the staff was overrun with other emergencies bumping my father's procedure.

Despite the expert's advice my mother's fears were growing intensely with the delays. Family and friends on being informed fully agreed in his decision, all imploring her to see the wisdom behind his determination: *"He could likely get cancer if he doesn't have this operation; is that what you want?"*

Of course my mother would never want that but her emotionality seemed more about her rather than what was best for my father, to the extent of disregarding the detail of his manhood on the line. He was to have the operation against my mother's protestations, her dread the last thing he needed.

♥   ♥

I arranged my flight around when it was thought my father was going into the hospital. With it postponed, my mother hoped I could change my ticket; it was non-refundable.

It had been thirteen years since I had last been to England—Su had joined me then for Andrea's son's Bar Mitzvah and generously offering to help with the cost—in preparation clarifying several times my wish to visit with my dearest Uncle Herbert and Auntie Enid at their condo on the beach at Bournemouth with a day or two on my own with them. Once their children had flown the coop to marry and have their own families, they saw fit to move to what had been their favorite romantic getaway. We had stayed in close phone contact, that not the same as us all together, naturally.

At every mention my mother indicated she agreed I have this chance, especially as Herbert was dealing with a seriously debilitating condition. In fact, I had a gnawing suspicion it might be the last time I saw him.

While organizing the week's plan my mother shot her forceful arrow. I was no more going to have this solo visit than the many of other wants she damned. Making the lame excuse of not seeing Herbert and Enid that much—they always had an open invitation at their place, and they coming to London often—I was astounded as she and my father had promised me this.

"You have no idea how much you've hurt me."

I did not hold my breath from telling my parents this once, yet it seemingly went in one ear and out the other.

Never mind. I swore they would not have a chance of ruining this trip for me, which meant I would have to let my mother have her way. In fact, having an extended line of credit I insisted on the purchase not just for train tickets, but to cover dinner at one of the finest Italian restaurants in the theatre district and my treat to our seeing the stage production of *Singing in the Rain*, if only for the pretense of control and steadiness of mind for the duration. (Of course, my expenses got away from me and I am still paying off my debt.)

Herbert, until the last minute, was unaware she and my father were staying overnight, their spare room easily accommodating. She sneakily suppressed the fact of my returning to London the following day, yet without return tickets—I assumed those I got at the kiosk were sufficient; my mother was rushing us to board the train and only later did I realize I had not collected them all.

We spent a beautiful afternoon walking the pier, a brisk wind taunting the vibrant sun. As the evening shade fell we toasted in reflection, enjoying the elaborate meal Enid prepared. The view from the living room window of the moon's sparkle across the water mesmerizing, I was so grateful to finally be there.

Early the next morning Herbert drove me to the depot to purchase return tickets. It meant a great deal to me talking in private—he and Enid had long known of the emotional distance between me and my mother—I told him how very much I had wanted to stay another day....

His expression was one of devastation. He adored me, always assuring me of his love. He could not hide his joy at finally holding me and now he was hearing from out of the blue that I was leaving already![8]

♥   ♥

My father had the surgery subsequent to my trip. It went fine but while being moved to recovery he suffered a heart attack; it was minor, thank God, yet answering the premonition of my mother. She deciphered changes in his memory, extremely frustrated at the need for repeating herself. His obstinate tantrums signaled his aggravation.

Unquestionably, such traits had been evidenced in their sixty-one-year marriage, yet my mother fought any real adjustment to his behavior while adamantly blaming his change on a brief loss of oxygen before he was able

---

8   A year almost to the day, Herbert died on February 19, 2013.

to be resuscitated. He had failed her. She poured on the dramatic, *"He's not the same man I fell in love with!"*

During the next three years he directed his efforts to rehabilitative therapies that would help boost his mental stimulation, which included his joy of crossword puzzles. He was far from lost. Panic, however, was building inside my mother who in the summer of 2015 demanded I come to England. I did not have the money; had there not been thousands of miles between us it may have been feasible, but I still could not have stayed for an indefinite period. I needed to keep my job.

She knew well my circumstances, yet I was on the hot seat to explain in futility. I heard nothing in the way of understanding, nor any offer to help pay for the flight. Half a dozen times repeating *"I cannot"*—she was not alone as other relatives and friends were there at immediate call—I could say no more, hanging up the phone, but not before her last words, *"You'll never forgive yourself."* She could only drill guilt for which I had none.

It had not gone unnoticed that my father was dealing with some dementia, more often forgetting my name. Every week I called and my mother answered the phone; passing it to him I could hear her reiterate, *"It's your daughter."* He came on brightly, after a few nudges. *"Hello, how are you?"*

My mother chose to place him in a hospice facility. I imagine that was quite saddening. Two months later, on November 22, 2015 at age eighty-seven, my beloved father died.

I am not encumbered by an ounce of doubt that he questioned the depth of my love for him, I forever peaceful in this knowledge.

A renaissance man, these verses quantifying his life:

"To thine own self be true."

—Hamlet

"'Tis better to have loved and lost than never to have loved at all."

—Alfred Lord Tennyson

CHAPTER 18

*W*hat is the purpose of my hardship when so much promise for a good quality of life looked certain? Wanting to seek understanding for promoting growth was my saving grace. For my mother to put other's opinions as foremost meant she was not truly present. One thing is for certain, I was not born self-loathing.

My father tried to fight the dysfunction, through his genuine efforts bringing a priceless normality. Showing me his support affirmed his deep love. Had it not been for his respect of my qualities and spirited authenticity I might be witless.

To fathom my mother's discordant inclination of which she has convinced herself justified remains difficult if not impossible. In my sixty-one years, many with my foothold interrupted, finally eureka! I am in full discernment that *her ways* cannot be attributed to anything truly about me.

I wanted to believe a day would come when I would feel my mother cease her undervaluation. I finally know that is not a viable hope. Now, at age eighty-six, she is still superior, shadowing humility. I am a woman of substance yet she withholding of compliments.

Motherhood is creating an individual. Individuality is deserving of celebration! Being callous and judgmental prevented my mother from absolute love for me. I remain someone she's never truly known.

My insightful nature is the sustenance driving my survival. With my struggles growing up the congregation's awareness was not on me but in relation to my father, its lasting impression I the Cantor's daughter. I can easily designate my being the black sheep of our family, I feeling my own course in my real time even as my twists and turns did not meet an expected design.

As a young girl my dreams for my life looked like most of my gender, wanting a happy marriage and children. After divorcing I considered other options. I had long believed that I would never mother a child in the manner by which I was, but once in my forties and having not found Mr. Right, I was feeling less capable, settling in fear of jeopardizing a healthy development.

♥   ♥

For all intents and purposes, my mother conducted her life as if the world revolved around her, her perception locked in self-absorption around her feelings. My brother, Warren, meant the world to me yet any comparison to her loss she deems unfair.

When Herbert passed away and I called my mother to express my condolences I anticipated her reciprocating in kind, she knowing the degree of love he had for me. She could only respond with *well that's what happens in life,* before diverting from this subject and my feelings in one swoop.

She is entirely responsible for the life she created. Apart from their passion my father's relationship with her was grounded in dependency, her desperate neediness. Just like her inability to embrace her daughter's love, she could not show him the gratitude he deserved. Rather than her conscious implementation of strength, a barometer from which happiness and success can rise, she imported the effortless route of repression.

With Herbert and my father now gone, my mother reinforces her bemoaning, *"Everyone else has family close by except me."* In fact, she has family nearby lovingly willing to help at a moment's notice but hesitates to bother them unless the need is urgent. Far across the pond there is but me maintaining my life. Yet onto me, in less than the best circumstances, having not the benefit of familial closeness, she permits thoughtless bother from an outlook of distort.

Her divestment of emotional support towards me not sufficiently plaguing, electing to physically separate illuminated a further sense of abandonment. It is time for my focus to be not on my mother deliberating on what she feels but on what matters to me. Beyond my lucidity to comprehend my truth, essential is the action I take on my best behalf and my stopping of automatic guilt-laden apologies.

It seems sinful spending one's life unsatisfied.

♥   ♥

Our principle assignment while on earth is learning to love who we are, mentally, emotionally and spiritually.

While physical abuse evidences scars, mental and emotional battery leaves the insidious psychic wounding. To consider it possible that we choose our parents may be hard, yet I believe there is a grand purpose by The Almighty (if at times seemingly crazy) in aligning us to the environment we inherit upon entrancing this universe, because of the essential promise of it bearing the fruit of our fortitude. The intrinsic purpose of gifting life surely cannot be solely burdening our existence in ceaseless suffrage; if that were the case, life would be worthless.

It is unconscionable the myriad of children disabled from the abuse received in the confines of home, which begs the philosophical question: *Why must the child justify the parent's intent on physically or mentally hurting them, with the resulting pain the duty of that child to overcome in order to save their life from complete ruination?*

To believe that our destiny is pre-ordained dismisses the critical recognition of choice in navigating the environment into which we are submerged. This is fate and we are powerless, we think. Seldom granted a life unwrinkled, the journey is this thicket of chaos where we either stay in avoidance of acknowledging our desires, or one where in trust we can trample time and again in refreshment of that space set for our flying, in wisdom our potential in our palms to our soul's magnificence.

♥   ♥

"What honestly matters isn't someone's perception, but critical is our recognition and advocacy of our true self. Courage trumps all other emotion, our lot in this life braved when we are being genuine."

—Original

"My first business is to so live that at least a few will
thank God that I lived when my little day is done."

—Alfred A. Montapert

♥   ♥

Within this memoir I have attempted emotional and factual authenticity.
The truth is that myriad have suffered far greater deprivation and sadness,
but every experience is profound in the particularity of its effect. My
purpose for sharing this journey began primarily as therapeutic. I also
am hopeful of it bearing an altruistic impact, through these meaningful
passages bolstering growth in children and adults toward the healthiest
capacities.

♥   ♥

Initiating the superb golden age of musical theatre was the successful
collaboration of Rogers and Hammerstein who infused Broadway's great
white way with masterful scores in the 1940s and 1950s.[9] From *The
Sound of Music* is the song "Climb Every Mountain," invoking the power
of belief that all one wishes to accomplish is within possibility:

> Climb every mountain
> Search high and low
> Follow every byway
> Every path you know
>
> Climb every mountain
> Ford every stream
> Follow every rainbow
> Till you find your dream
>
> A dream that will need
> All the love you can give
> Every day of your life
> For as long as you live

---

9   Richard Rogers was the composer and Oscar Hammerstein II the lyricist.

> Climb every mountain
> Ford every stream
> Follow every rainbow
> Till you find your dream

From *Carousel* is "You'll Never Walk Alone," which speaks to the belief that a higher power can lift us up from the depths of loneliness to true emancipation:

> When you walk through a storm
> Hold your head up high
> And don't be afraid of the dark
>
> At the end of a storm
> There's a golden sky
> And the sweet silver song of a lark
>
> Walk on through the wind
> Walk on through the rain
> Though your dreams be tossed and blown
>
> Walk on, walk on
> With hope in your heart
> And you'll never walk alone
> You'll never walk alone

♥   ♥

This is the history I lived as no one else could tell it. In deliverance of this production I liberate myself from the baggage of shame, of which my spirit believed it deserved ownership, in unequivocal declaration: *I love myself, dark spots and all!*

On the highest note, my concluding message:

> I've arrived and caught the brass ring! For the first time realizing what it truly feels like to be happy, conscious of the sense of inner contentment.
>
> The bold lesson reached: the self I first knew—my character's shape—is wiser from the complex tempo of experience.

*I Am A Loving, Compassionate
And Powerful Woman!*

It wouldn't have been my proclamation in Lifespring had
I not heard the voice reminding me of what I've known all
along. Experiencing the rebirth of my innate self, I stand a
winner over which, for too long, held so much influence. At
the place of my greatest capacity to set myself free of hurt,
pain and sadness, I'm embracing my opulence of being.

I'm handling with less stress, insecurity, life's daily events,
my trust empowered.

It's those outer world's influences that either make or break
that child's future. Life's grandeur excels as one is driven to
betterment in spite of it all. The only direction is forward,
life to be lived with confidence while owning imperfection.

♥   ♥

God lies in the details. Everyone on the planet can sculpt their best legacy
by yielding to their compassionate forces.

PART TWO

EPILOGUE

Five years into my methodical writing of this memoir, thoughts about my health were becoming a nagging worry. I had no specific reason to feel anxious, just the fact of my aging. I made this audacious pact with God: *Let me get it done and then you can take me if it is my time.*

While the opening scene depicts my father in a heartrending role consoling a congregant in the hospital, little did I know that a week subsequent to the eloquent finalization of this production it would be me on the gurney rushed through the doors to the emergency room seriously injured, I having been the pedestrian struck in a hit and run vehicular assault.

The pendulous irony of fate approbates inclusion of this epilogue.

♥　　　♥

My eyes penetrated the ceiling, which was the only direction accessible—a reminder of the hours I had spent in my bedroom when young, in a similar pose of fragility. My body crushed, I lay immobilized in pain at Harborview Medical Center, my mind suspended in the inconceivable reality of my circumstance as doctors and nurses situated a saline drip into a plump vein, scribed my blood pressure, lined me up for the head-to-toe CT imaging....

What seemingly was another summer beginning, to fly by without having taken an opportune vacation, would turn out, in 2017, to be an exceptionally long and memorable one, if far from pleasurable.

♥   ♥

Thursday would normally be my day off, but on the 1st of June I am keeping my promise to make up for one I previously missed. A hair late I am not worried. I am not rushing. I will stay as long as required.

At a few minutes after 10:00 o'clock in the morning, I am standing at the southeast corner of Spring Street and Third Avenue awaiting the light in my favor. I am dressed particularly pretty in a maxi navy and cream floral skirt, an elegant navy blouse spontaneously dug out from the rear of my closet where it hung forgotten, my chocolate brown blazer with coordinating sleek, mid-heel ankle boots, while my brief case doubling as a handbag swings from my right shoulder.

Old school, I am not distracted by earplugs or other paraphernalia, but extra cautious in my awareness of my surroundings, a habit due to recent sightings of increasing recklessness on the roads.

The light changes and I start out on the crosswalk, when to my horror the sky blue sedan is accelerating straight towards me at great speed!

I'm going to die...a split second thought, I should duck to effectuate the collision with my head...in another second, no; I want to live, I must keep moving.

I zoom in to capture the driver's face; I see it, or so I think, or is the windshield in actuality just glistening hues of red as reflected by the sun streaking through from the east—I believe now this a sign from God, sending light to lessen my fear—at once happening, the motion slowed.

Go around me, you have time...God help me...I can't get out of the way in time...I'm going down! As in a terrifying nightmare facing my own obliteration, extending my hand instinctively I imagine my supernatural might in preventing the inevitable.

I feel the velocity of the vehicle's impact smashing violently into the left side of my 5'3" frame as I am flung up onto the bumper and thrown out into the intersection thirty feet, landing flattened into the concrete in a fetal position.

Time stills yet my heart keeps beating; "*oh my God, oh my God,*" in every constricted gasp beseeching mercy.

My life didn't flash before my eyes, it isn't over!
Immediately people are gathering around, one lady kneeling near my ear wanting to give me comfort and calm any impulse she thinks I might have to move.

I am frozen in fear of my condition. The police now here, traffic is halted; full of questions, assessing my wounds...do I know my name, age, what happened? Bagging my wallet, keys, jewelry, cutting away my jacket, blouse...I hear the ambulance siren in fast approach.

I'm within a block from my downtown Seattle office! I can't shake my nerves...what about my boss? He's my friend, he'll be terribly worried...I can't work!

♥   ♥

My shoulder is destroyed I know it. *What about my arm, my back, my legs? How severe are my injuries?*

Prior to this event I never suffered a broken bone, nor had I ever required emergency hospitalization.

Now, with my shoulder in infinitesimal pieces, only one viable option offered any chances of restoring the use of my arm, but the doctors initially told me I would need to wait two weeks for the swelling to dissipate. *In such pain how can I possibly wait that long?*

I was moved out of the ICU the next morning to an assigned room in another wing. Having an abundance of time on my hands to ruminate through my shock on this event, remarkable was my feeling renewed transformative affirmations rising from the depths of my being.

Later that day the surgical team came in to inform me they would operate in three days, giving me a bit of relief.

My back had suffered fractures in both thoracic and lumbar spinal regions. The initial prognosis was two more operations were necessary. Fortune had me in its grasp with a determination of a different solution. Built to my unique measurement I would wear a Jewett brace—quite apropos—24/7 with the hopeful preservation against degeneration from my injuries.

My mother had to be told but I could not handle it. I felt untrusting of her capacity of focus as beneficial for my needs, knowing she would be the wreck requiring my consoling of her. In no uncertain terms would I accept her seizing the momentum for deflection from my near death. I handed off to admirable Leslie command of my wish that she apprize my mother of the specifics. Naturally, as she was unable to be at my side, I would have understood her nervous hesitation. In sisterhood she always a trooper was not about to feed her distress. She realized the need for stepping into the duty I gave her without complaint.

My first stop pre-surgery on Monday morning June 5th was to receive a numb block injection after which wheeled to the operating room, my sight locking on the fluorescence above, anesthesia consuming my consciousness.

Formally termed a "shoulder arthroplasty," it is a full replacement with the hardware implant extending from the socket to almost the elbow. Ten years earlier this surgery was in its infancy, but now being performed at the highest efficiency. With his team assisting my handsome surgeon cut a deep incision four and a half inches down the crease where my shoulder meets my chest.

♥   ♥

Smoothly becoming awake after two hours on the table, I burst into tears in overwhelming joy at my survival of this horrendous crime.

I could contemplate a positive future looming close.

Once sutured my whole arm was secured in a sling to prevent any movement. The numb block continued for several days; in the process of it lessening, the after effect was my chest and neck and all the way down my left arm becoming puffed with a charcoal dissipation that my body eventually would eliminate.

As my hemoglobin count was quite low, a few days later the doctors ordered a blood transfusion to take four hours. No problem, I was not going anywhere; maybe I could be told my blood type—I had long been curious to know this very important piece of information and learning of it as "B+" as in be positive. *Yes, I can run with that!*

Not until I finally stood up after about ten days did I realize I would have to learn to walk again. Incredibly, at first with the cane, I could use the bedside commode and move around a few feet, while my medication monitoring machines and saline drip were now strategically situated on a portable contraption. Succeeding to increased steps once around the floor then several times, the nurses and aides commending my graduation, in a little over a week I was showing agility of speed and balance that precipitated my transfer to a rehabilitation facility.

While in the hospital three weeks my friend Bruce was a great help. Witnessing my colorless complexion and weakened condition in the first days he did his best in cheering me up with regular visits and calls and handling my apartment issues while holding in check his emotions. For all of his support I will always be grateful.

♥   ♥

In my first week at Park West Nursing & Rehab in West Seattle I powered through, taking longer walks each day, before a physical therapist was assigned. Since my shoulder would take several weeks to heal before that area would partner into my regimen, she structured a plan around my lower extremities to incorporate ballet steps. I could not have been happier renewing my use of this art.

My hope was that I could leave in one more week, for I anxiously wanted to get back to the comfort of my home. I was demonstrating the highest degree of improvements, my flexibility surprising even the austere on staff.

I proved my eligibility for discharge, with the 4th of July my personal return to independence.

A month to the day subsequent to the arthroplasty I was freed from the sling entrapping my arm. Amazingly, as my left elbow to my hand had been saved from damage, I had the maneuverability with many tasks with my right arm taking the greater weight. In just eight weeks, my range higher and wider gifted a freshness of winning. Since word processing is the mainstay of my employment, I was able to return two months post-collision.

It is miraculous that my mental faculties were not imperiled, no brain damage, no concussion. I did sustain massive deep tissue bruising throughout my body. Noticeably, when my head hit the pavement a huge hematoma formed creating an indentation of my scalp; my calf also swelled in a mass of dark purple to black shades, these symptoms to take a month before healing.

With respect to my vertebrae injuries, three months to the day of the crime the x-rays showed the stabilization of my spinal fractures resulting in the welcome news that I could relieve myself from the brace.

In all honesty, I could not have asked for a greater ministering of care from the surgical team or therapeutic personnel. From the cleaning crew to the food servers up the chain of specialties, I am profoundly thankful for their outpouring of compassion and praise. Initially holding me to the recognition of how vital going forward would be my own efforts taking in stride discomfort, with sustaining mobility their sentiments are still resonating.

Maintaining a slim weight my entire life with healthy eating and daily walks as exercise, I feel, helped equip my body's infrastructure, reducing catastrophic disablement.

What cannot be negated is that I am changed from this harrowing experience, my aluminum implant creating residual emotional reminders.

♥　　　♥

Why does the human condition render an individual helpless to proper communication of honest feelings in the everyday, only the near death event sparking the need for such demonstration?

I know I have a lot of love surrounding me, prayers abounding. Yet, the lack of demonstrative displays by the very people, my family, who claim their greatest affection, surprised, they finding it unnecessary going the extra mile to send cards and flowers, for which usual such an event. Just another wake-up bell to my family's odd manner, but all comparisons aside, my life experiences teaching me to value the totality of that gifted, even if it is in words only.

My healing had put me in a better frame of mind for contacting my mother. Elation was in her voice as she let the best of her heart be exposed: *"I love you so very much and I'm tremendously proud of you. You're so brave and doing so well in your recovery so far...."*

Where, during my past, I could not help but feel my mother's affection as feckless, the rarity of words loving to my heart thin in fulfillment, she had turned a corner in her desire for pathos. In the six months following, our weekly conversations would draw a mutual sensitivity.

♥　　　♥

I lost my mother on December 8, 2017. She barely carried on after my father died and often spoke of wishing to be with him. A succession of falls and unwillingness to pursue proper medical attention prevented recovery, thus adding to her susceptibility for another, which occurred.

Since several calls to her home had gone unanswered the police were summoned, breaking down the door finding her in a catatonic state on the floor.

My connection with my cousins had waned due to distance. It was from Julian—the name of John Lennon's son, this date concurrent to the murder of his father—that I received the news and upon whom I now depended for help with her burial. My mother had been especially close to him, in a pinch a source of support.

With embarrassment I revealed to Julian the truth about my parents not articulating the details of how their affairs should be handled after they were gone. They had deemed such information not fit for me, thus I without the power or means to contribute.

In the days that ensued my mother's will was made available—my father did not make one. Having no idea, it has surprised her bequeathing a mere one-quarter of her estate to her only living offspring, with the rest designated to two charities.

In Hebrew the word is *tzedakah*, and although this commandment to help those less fortunate was a major priority in my parents' lives, such benevolence which should start with one's offspring did not translate in my direction.

My mother stayed beguiling with a methodical determination. She could not bring herself the bestowing onto me her highest generosity. With ignorance of her shortcomings, I would remain responsible for having not quite measured up to her satisfaction.

I traveled to England in October 2018 to attend her stone setting. A prayer service took place prior to viewing the grave sight in the cemetery chapel, conducted by her great-nephew, a rabbi. As he reflected lovingly upon his childhood memories I stood there numb, feeling invisible.

The irony not lost on me, the attribute my mother left for them to memorialize was one of martyr, her strategy. A woman who carried on with acts of kindness, despite great suffering, especially showering Herbert's grandchildren with gifts beyond their childhood; they left to cherish her legacy as pious.

I hope the reader does glean my forgiveness of my mother. Yet, I will not forget for it is through my insight to discerning her motives that I have found the strength and allowance for my soul's expansion.

♥   ♥

Providence seemed at play in my mother's final hour. Nana's and Daddy Low's passing, a decade apart, occurred during Chanukah in the month of Kislev. The date my mother died also corresponds on the Judaic calendar with that of her parents and my father, who preceded her by two years and sixteen days. This heavenly rejoining is, I feel, not simply coincidental but the blessing of divinity.

As the last of my immediate family I feel complete. My days yet to come, my time just begun, I am rejoicing in the Lord. My emotional shackles unlocked, I can freely set sail on my grandest destiny.

♥   ♥

In more than two years since this crime the suspect has been successful in evading apprehension. The police investigation is still open, yet despite witness accounts, a bus video, my appearance on KIRO TV and the case on Crime Stoppers of Puget Sound, a cosmic glitch hampers its solvability: the car registration was left in the previous owner's name leaving the driver's identity a mystery.

I was without health insurance when this collision happened but, thank God, I was relieved to learn the Washington State Crime Victims Compensation Program was taking charge of paying all of my bills.

I will my centering throughout my days forthcoming in opposition of bitterness. *This is the higher blessing, my reward is my life!* The need to be forgiving is ever present. For every painful event impacting my life I erase any idea that I contain the power to control its assault.

On the surface it can surprise no one, that dance of anger, but it is precisely when our negativity is heightened that we hold the human capacity for its temperance. It is from this character strength that we create the space for praise in the beautification of each day, for recognition of a unity with all species, for a realization of God's greater purpose extant, if not readily understood.

♥   ♥

Leslie gave me a prayer pendant a few years back. Not wearing it often, I chose to that day I was hit. Inside it I had placed not some biblical verse, but the chorus of a Cindy Lauper song, it rousing the ethereal:

If you're lost you can look
And you will find me
Time after time
If you fall I will catch you
I will be waiting
Time after time

I was not alone that day. Cradling me I believe my lost loved ones, my surviving their reinforcement from beyond.

In celebration of the anniversary my appreciation overflows. I am tremendously fortunate to have overcome my difficult recovery. My value is renewed for all that I am and all I have accomplished. Hallelujah!

The pulse of time in my fourth quarter is calling me into action, not inertia. Victory is my resilience as I rise up to embrace the bigger picture with grace. A child of God, I am granted an impenetrable countenance. My spirit holds a youthful perseverance and a willing of fresh dreams for the asking.

Nurturing my sensibility, integrity and self-respect, I live evermore joyfully, with the conviction to cultivate new relationships.

That humans are fallible is an unallowable excuse for betraying our quintessential purpose to do no harm, to avoid judgment, gossip, all of the emotional malignancy. Rather, our duty with our humanity is guardian to our inner angel, the source of honesty guiding a minimum of vanity but that maximum of positive intention.

With God as our heart guide we uphold His trust in becoming the evolution of our best self.

TRIBUTES

I am grateful to my parents and extended family for their blessed gifts of affection, as well as hard lessons.

To my dearest friend, Leslie (Goldberg) Byrne, I will always be thankful for her love and unceasing loyalty that only continues to grow, making my life resplendent.

I am fortunate for another close friend, Bruce Wolf, for his understanding and generosity over many years.

My heart will forever hold the memories of my three impassioned friends Terrence Smith, Robin Pavlosky and Joseph Ranft, their amazing talents and vast contributions to the world tragically too brief.

In the beginning was God, today is God,
Tomorrow will be God.

Who can make an image of God?
He has no body.

He is the word which comes out of your mouth.
That word!

It is no more, it is past, and still it lives!
So is God.

—Traditional African Tribal Prayer

www.ingramcontent.com/pod-product-compliance
Lightning Source LLC
Chambersburg PA
CBHW021828090426
42811CB00032B/2073/J